PRAIS

WHAT I WISH MY MOTHER
HAD TOLD ME ABOUT MARRIAGE

Greg and Julie Gorman have written an honest, candid and authentic book that is a must-read for every marriage.
Les Parrott, Ph.D.
Author of *Saving Your Marriage Before It Starts*

Julie and Greg have opened the window to their home and their hearts for others to see that only a marriage fully surrendered to God, and lived out by the power of the Holy Spirit, can flourish in this fallen world. The transparency and vulnerability this couple is willing to expose gives evidence to the healing and restoration God has done in their own marriage, and to the hope that is possible for yours.
Carmen Pate
Principal with Alliance Ministries

The Gorman's have a special way of getting to the heart of the matter in language we all understand. Their insights force us to re-think our notions of marriage, and challenge us to raise God's standard in all of our relationships.
James Randall Robison
LIFE Today TV

Greg and Julie deliver timeless truths and incredible insights to unleash greater intimacy in marriage.
Shannon Ethridge
Life Coach and Author of the million-copy best-selling *Every Woman's Battle* series

This book is full of profound wisdom packaged in a wonderfully easy-to-read way: picture friends who have been through a lot sitting down with you over coffee, and transparently sharing some vital things that will make a difference in your marriage. And they *will* make a difference, because the content is fantastic. Their focus is on surrendering to God, dwelling in prayer, and communicating with your spouse—and *how* to do those things. In all my research, I have seen that the power of faith in marriage isn't just "helpful" but *essential* to creating the truly long-lasting, selfless, and happy marriage we all long for. Bravo to Greg and Julie for this wonderful book.

Shaunti Feldhahn
Social Researcher and Best-selling Author of *For Women Only* and *The Surprising Secrets of Highly Happy Marriages*

As young girls we dreamed of growing up and getting married. It all seemed like a fairy tale filled with "happily ever afters." Then we got married and realized that *happily* didn't always come *easily*. *What I Wish My Mother Had Told Me about Marriage* lovingly brings the truth to light about both the challenges and blessings of marriage. In their unique, inspirational style, Greg and Julie Gorman help us realize the joy of this sacred union, and show us how to glorify God through our relationship with our spouse.

Karol Ladd
Author of *The Power of a Positive Wife*

Julie and Greg have written an honest, powerful, and biblical book on marriage. If your marriage is in trouble, don't do anything drastic until you've taken the time to read their book. With conviction and humility, Julie and Greg dare to go after the issues that all too often destroy what could otherwise be a thriving, beautiful marriage.

Susie Larson
National Radio Host, Speaker, Author of *Your Beautiful Purpose*

From sharing dreams in life to sharing intimacy in the bedroom, Greg and Julie divulge the secrets to creating connection and devotion as God designed for your marriage relationship.

Tammy Maltby
Speaker, Emmy Award-winning TV Cohost and Author of *Confessions of a Good Christian Girl* and *The God Who Sees You*

Everything about this book is to love, love, love—from Greg and Julie's honest sharing to the thought-provoking questions and Scriptures they pose that will challenge you to think deeply about your own marriage. Keep a highlighter handy—I particularly enjoyed the "letters from God" that helped me spiritually process each of the ten "secrets" highlighted by the authors. Get a copy for every married and engaged couple you know. This book is a keeper!

Lorraine Pintus
Writing Coach, Author of *Jump Off the Hormone Swing*

Greg and Julie Gorman are honest and transparent as they pull back the curtain on their marriage and show you from their own mistakes and experiences what it takes to beat the odds and fall back in love with your spouse. You'll enjoy this journey back to your spouse's heart. And you'll want to take it over and over again as Greg and Julie encourage you, strengthen you, give you hope, and make you laugh.

Cindi and Hugh McMenamin
Co-authors of *When Couples Walk Together: 31 Days to a Closer Connection*

I am so grateful Greg and Julie wrote this book! These hard-learned lessons will steer all of us to more meaningful relationships and stronger marriages. I love the real-life honesty coupled with big splashes of fun that fill up every page.

Brady Boyd
Senior Pastor, New Life Church, Author of *Addicted to Busy*

Read this book with an open heart to God and a stubbornness to fight for your marriage. Julie and Greg Gorman write candidly about how they have overcome many difficulties in marriage—and how you can too.

Arlene Pellicane
Author of *31 Days to Becoming a Happy Wife*

Reading Greg and Julie Gorman's book is like standing in a gray courtyard as slight rays of sunshine slowly pierce through a thick cloud cover, eventually splitting the sky with a light so fulfilling and so warm, quickly changing things. I commend them for such clear thinking on such a cloudy subject within the community of faith.

Dennis Mansfield
Author of *Beautiful Nate* and *Finding Malone*

WHAT I WISH MY MOTHER HAD TOLD ME ABOUT MARRIAGE

UNLOCKING 10 SECRETS
to a Thriving Marriage

GREG AND JULIE GORMAN

Authentic

What I Wish My Mother Had Told Me About Marriage
Copyright © 2014 Greg and Julie Gorman

Cover design by Peter Gloege | Look Design
Cover photo by Denkou Images | SuperStock
Internal design by Rob Williams | InsideOut Design
Edited by Dean Merrill

Published by Authentic Publishers
188 Front Street, Suite 116-44
Franklin, TN 37064

Authentic Publishers is a division of Authentic Media, Inc.

Library of Congress Cataloging-in-Publication Data

Gorman, Greg and Julie
What I Wish My Mother Had Told Me About Marriage :
unlocking 10 secrets to a thriving marriage / Greg and Julie Gorman
p. cm.
ISBN 978-1-78078-127-3
978-1-78078-260-7 (e-book)

Printed in the United States of America

21 20 19 18 17 16 15 14   10 9 8 7 6 5 4 3 2 1

CONTENTS

FOREWORD

*[The Spirit] will not tolerate in you the self-sins
even though they are permitted and excused by most
Christians. By the self-sins I mean self-love, self-pity,
self-seeking, self-confidence, self-righteousness,
self-aggrandizement, self-defense . . .*

A.W. TOZER, *THE PURSUIT OF MAN*

The "self-sins."

If I had to pick a phrase to describe the problem Julie and Greg Gorman are tackling in this book, that's the one I'd choose.

The apostle Paul tackled the same issue from a slightly different angle. "When I was a child," he wrote, "I talked like a child, I thought like a child, I reasoned like a child. When I became a man, I put childish ways behind me" (1 Corinthians 13:11).

Let's face it. Growing up is a process of realizing that "it's *not* all about me." And nowhere is this more obvious—or more crucial to success and happiness—than in the arena of marriage. You can keep the focus on yourself long past your twenty-first birthday and still get along *pretty* well as long as you're flying solo. It's when you vow to enter into a "one-flesh" union with another human being that things can get a little dicey—*if* you haven't figured out how to shift your orientation and leave the old childish ways behind.

Greg and Julie know all about this. They learned their lessons in the school of hard knocks. As Julie will tell you in the very first chapter, she can remember a time when their marriage didn't seem to stand a chance. *Why does every conversation end in an argument?* she thought one night as she lay crying her eyes out on the bedroom floor. *Why can't we go a single day without fighting? Why do we brawl around like a couple of children?* As it turned out, the answers to her questions had a lot to do with what Tozer called the "self-sins."

Julie and Greg have since learned how to overcome those obstacles. More than that, they've gone on to build a strong, vital, thriving, and mutually satisfying marriage. But it wasn't easy, and they were only able to make it happen by taking an honest look at their personal wants and expectations, and facing up to that harsh reality the Scriptures describe as "dying to *self*."

The contents of *What I Wish My Mother Had Told Me About Marriage* are the fruit of that gritty experience. The authors have written it all down because they care about people like *you*. But don't worry—there's nothing harsh or condemning about their message. They aren't here to blame or lecture anyone. If your relationship with your spouse is floundering, you'll get nothing but compassion, support, and understanding from them. They know what it's like because they've been there. That's why they have such a deep and sincere desire to help other struggling couples shorten the road to marital transformation.

And make no mistake about it. *Transformation* is what they're all about. *Transformation* through surrendering to God, a forgiving attitude, and taking responsibility for your own actions. *Transformation* through sensitivity to spiritual warfare, genuine concern for each other's best interests, and mature self-control. *Transformation* through intentionality in the areas of intimacy, personal growth, and shared dreams. *Transformation* through deciding to promote someone else's happiness over your own.

The journey to transformation begins when you turn the page.

Dr. Greg Smalley
Vice President, Family Ministries, Focus on the Family

A Note from the Authors

Dear friend,

Being married is truly one of the greatest joys of our life . . . but we didn't always feel that way. At one time, we wondered why God instituted marriage. At weddings we wanted to shout, "Don't do it!" We truly wondered if any marriage could last.

So as you read through the following pages and allow us to enter into your living room, your home, and heart, we promise to treat you kindly. Our hope is to provide practical and spiritual truths that move you towards greater intimacy in your marriage. Whether you are newly engaged and preparing for your wedding day or you've been married for fifty years, you'll discover ten secrets to make your marriage thrive.

If you love being married, we pray you find additional ways to enhance your relationship. If your marriage is struggling, we pray God provides you with life-transforming insights that invite His restoration. Jesus promised, "A bruised reed he will not break, and a smoldering wick he will not snuff out, till he leads justice to victory."[1] Further, God declares He is "close to the brokenhearted and saves those who are crushed in spirit."[2]

The truth is, every person—male or female, young or old, single or married—innately longs to love *someone* and to have that *someone* love them back. Oftentimes, we walk through life hoping for an unconditional acceptance of who we are. Though we may never ask audibly, everything in us shouts, "Do you love me—the real me? Will you accept the person I truly am?" Though Mr. or Mrs. Perfect may not exist, and the "happily-ever-after" we experience may look radically different than we first envisioned, we may just discover as we surrender our dreams to God that He gives us a mate far better than any fairy tale book could depict. Thus, our story begins!

What I Wish My Mother Had Told Me about Marriage contains ten secrets we wish we had heard long ago. The truth is, our moms didn't really talk about what marriage would be like for us. Especially back in that time (the 1970s and '80s), we all just *assumed* (dangerous word!) that all would run smoothly. If you've read Julie's first book, you already know that her early adult life didn't work out that way at all. We've traveled a long and winding road to get to the point of grasping what this book now offers to you.

Each chapter contains encouragement under these headings: *A Moment for Preparation, A Powerful Truth, Questions to Ask, Verses to Consider, A Letter from the Father, Closing Prayer, Greg's Turn,* and additional closers called *For Your Reflection* and *A Practical Application.* Please don't rush your way through these chapters; don't feel as if you need to "conquer" this book in a certain length of time. Instead, give yourself permission to reflect, to answer questions honestly, to pray the prayers, even to re-read a section to gain further understanding.

You can read this book by yourself, or as a couple, or within a group. We pray the practical applications and biblical insights will inspire life transformation as you read powerful testimonies from us along with many other brave men and women. We hope that by sharing our mistakes you will avoid them, and by sharing what brought about our victories you will find surprising truths to make your marriage thrive.

But before we begin, we need to pause. Perhaps you're asking yourself the question we once did: "Can our marriage truly be healed?" If so, let us assure you that the answer is yes! Not only can it be restored, it can be transformed into a beautiful partnership filled with love and respect. Let your hope be renewed. You can experience healing. Your marriage can be saved. You can experience an emotionally healthy family. Your children can be spared from a dysfunctional legacy. Trust can be established. Gentleness can rule your home. Peace can reign in your heart and mind.

Remember, as long as you have breath, it is never too late for God to restore. May He bless you as you read.

GREG AND JULIE GORMAN

ACKNOWLEDGMENTS

To our heavenly Father, thank You! We live to bring You glory. Thank You for calling us to Your service and for healing our marriage. Without You, we are nothing. Thank You for being the One constant in our marriage, for running after us, for forgiving us. Father, breathe Your life into this message. Anoint it with Your Spirit. And accomplish all You promised. We have nothing to give You except what You have given us, but we gladly offer You all we are and all we have. We love You!

Special appreciation goes to Lorraine Pintus, Anne Bosworth, and Greg's mom, Donna English; thank you for your support and for reading and re-reading countless revisions to help clarify the message of this book.

To our agent, Kyle Duncan, and the Authentic publishing team, thanks for your continued support and belief in us and for doing everything in your power to share this life-transforming message. It is our joy to partner with you.

To Julie's sister and her husband, Rose and Dennis Balgavy, you both are incredibly gifted. Thank you for your prayers and for investing the countless hours it took to organize, create, record, and edit the videos correlating with each chapter of this book, and for the tremendous book trailer you created. We can only imagine what your mansion will look like when we get to heaven!

To the real-life people whose stories appear in this book—even though we didn't use your actual names. We wanted to protect your privacy and that of your family. But the essentials of your experience have not been altered, and we know they will be helpful to enrich the perceptions of many readers.

Special thanks to Julie's mom, Marie Ely, and Greg's stepmom and mom, Sue Gorman and Donna English, for all the truths you did teach us. Thank you for your love.

To our children, Courtney, Sommer, and Joshua—we hope we will pass down and always live out before you every surprising truth contained in this book. May your marriages thrive and be filled with absolute joy! May your children and their children continually carry a legacy of Christlike character and love. Your lives bring us so much joy and laughter. We love you.

A Moment for Preparation

Transformation arises not through ambition or self-will but amidst our surrender to the One who holds all things together through His Word. Generally, we don't take steps toward growth until the pain of staying the same exceeds the pain of change. Only in that place does true surrender begin.

The esteemed pastor and author A. W. Tozer once wrote, "The reason why many are still troubled, still seeking, still making little forward progress is because they haven't yet come to the end of themselves."[1]

How about you? Are you striving? Wrestling? Feeling overwhelmed or powerless? If so, silence your thoughts. Quiet your emotions. Relinquish your control and release the outcome of your concerns to God. Entrust your life and marriage to Him by simply praying, "Lord, I choose to put my trust in You. Help me. Reveal Yourself to me in every part of my life."

SURRENDER, COMPLETELY

"Come to me, all you who are weary and burdened,
and I will give you rest. Take my yoke upon you
and learn from me, for I am gentle and humble in heart."

MATTHEW 11:28-29

I'd already been through one divorce. I couldn't believe I was contemplating another.

"What's wrong with me?" I wailed. "Why can't any man love me like I want to be loved?" The walls closed in around me that evening. My heart ached. I cried for what seemed like hours, though the big red numbers on the nightstand clock reflected only fifteen minutes.

While lying prostrate on the floor, my eyes fixated on the vast number of dust bunnies beneath my bed. Huhhhhh! I let out a long exhausted sigh and thought, *Great! One more thing I need to get done.*

Then . . . a peculiar silence began to surround me. I considered how, only thirty minutes prior, Greg and I had been laughing and joking together. And then, BAM! Our thoughts had collided like two semis smashing head-on. *Why did every conversation end in an argument? Why couldn't we go a single day without fighting? Why did we brawl like a couple of children?* The relentless questions bombarded my mind.

"Stop!" I screamed. *Oh, would my mind ever just stop?* I wondered to myself, *Why can't Greg understand that all I want is for him to want to be with me? Did he really mean he couldn't live like this anymore? Will he come back?*

I curled into a fetal position and pulled my white king-sized pillow to the floor. I pressed it hard against my face, and for a moment I sniffed in the freshness of the orange blossom fabric softener. But my freshly washed sheets were no match for my tireless fears. *Now what? If Greg doesn't come back, what will life be like for our newborn daughter and my five-year-old stepdaughter? What will I do if he really does leave me?*

I had never felt more helpless, afraid, or alone. Weak and trembling, I softly whispered, "Please, Lord, please, Father, fix it! I don't know who's right or who's wrong anymore, and I don't care. Change me. Change him. Just do whatever it takes to fix us." My desperation to save my marriage superseded every other desire.

My head throbbed. My eyes swelled. All my pride poured out along with the painful tears. I was truly at the end of "me."

Just when I felt as though I couldn't take another breath, God's comforting warmth covered me from head to toe. You know that feeling where time stands still and every hair on your body stands to full attention? I felt a keen awareness that God had heard my prayers. I'm not sure how God does what He does, but within a few short minutes, His irresistible peace replaced my desperation. I went from feeling completely hopeless to sensing God's assurance that He would fix my marriage.

However, laced within His promise was an expectation requiring my complete surrender—a surrender not contingent on my husband's worthiness but God's. He extended His invitation with three simple questions:

Will you exchange your self-serving love for My sacrificial love?

"Yes, Lord."

Will you reject society's standards of love and extend My unconditional love to Greg?

Again, I replied, "Yes, Lord. I will."

Will you entrust Greg to Me?

With a slight pause, I really considered what God was asking, but then quickly responded with full conviction, "Yes, Lord, I will."

God's questions revealed a crucial secret every married couple must adopt, and an invitation every couple must accept.

A Powerful Truth

Secret #1—The key to experiencing a thriving marriage is our complete surrender to God.

What is surrender?

Is it mindless obedience? Self-abasing martyrdom? Is it a decision based on convenience? Is it a simple choice that comes instantaneously?

No, not at all.

Surrender isn't reliant on our ability or reasoning. Surrender isn't contingent on our spouse's merit. Surrender isn't something we do when it's opportune or convenient. Surrender is a lifestyle and constant choice, an intentional decision to put our hope, confidence, and faith in God alone.

We see glimpses of this faith in the scriptural account of Shadrach, Meshach, and Abednego. As the three young Hebrew men faced the fury of Nebuchadnezzar, they resolved to not bow to his idol of gold. They said, "O Nebuchadnezzar, we do not need to defend ourselves before you in this matter. If we are thrown into the blazing furnace, the God we serve is *able* to save us from it, and he *will* rescue us from your hand, O king. But even if he does not, we want you to know, O king, that we will not serve your gods or worship the image of gold you have set up."[2]

Did you catch it?

Shadrach, Meshach, and Abednego demonstrated full confidence in God's ability but lived in a state of abandonment to His will. At no point did they indicate doubt. They showed no need to defend themselves. They stood firm and resolved to do what was right, regardless of the outcome.

Do you live with that much abandonment in your marriage? Are you content to let God defend you? Are you fully trusting in His ability?

Surrender invites the limitless power of God to *show up* and *show off* in our lives and marriages!

Faith means that even when our circumstances dictate hopelessness, we remain hopeful, because God can be trusted.

Surrender may sound like the Christian thing to do . . . but *understanding* it and *doing* it are worlds apart.

That night, as I laid prostrate on our off-white carpeted bedroom floor, God asked me to surrender my control for His, my self-will for His Spirit-filled living, my rights for His idea of a servanthood posture (basin and towel), my incessant need to protect for an abandoned understanding that He would be my protector. His call to surrender challenged me to love Greg as He had loved me.

It was time for God's Love Lesson 101.

You see, Greg and I had fallen into a whirlwind courtship and married six short months after meeting. Although I failed to recognize it at the time, I carried hidden scars from the emotional, physical, and sexual abuse I had experienced as a child, and I unknowingly placed my need for validation and security upon Greg. I had no idea just how much I needed to surrender my needs to God. My extreme insecurities and incessant need to control opposed every fiber of Greg's carefree, fun-loving disposition.

I fired out questions like a machine gun.

"Where are you going?"

"Who's going along?"

"When will you be home?"

Seems innocent enough, right? Unfortunately, each question sprang from a place of suspicion and need to control. My fear of being hurt caused an insatiable need to protect myself from harm.

My inability to surrender to God caused constant friction. In the early years of our marriage, Greg and I fought more days than not. Our confrontations often began in the early evening and lasted to the wee hours of the morning. Rash words spoken in a moment's emotional flare left us both wounded.

"Baby, I just want you to want to be here with me! Why do you always want to be gone? Can't you see what I need? Don't you care?"

Over time, Greg's concessions to stay home with me grew old. Eventually, he tired of my clinginess and retaliated by asserting his independence.

Another day, another fight!

It seemed I knew how to push Greg's buttons, but didn't know how *not* to. My needs constantly pushed Greg to his limit, as his drove me to mine.

I conditioned my love according to Greg's actions. My emotions teetered on his approval or the lack thereof.

Surrender my needs to God? I thought I had. I mean, I loved God; I wanted to please Him. The problem was just how blind I was to the whole situation.

Have you ever been so short-sighted that every argument seemed to be someone else's fault? Have you ever experienced a need so great that it prevented you from comprehending your spouse's needs? Have you ever been frustrated because you had no idea how to avoid pushing your spouse's buttons?

"If I put my trust in human beings first, I will end in despairing of everyone; I will become bitter, because I have insisted on man being what no man can ever be— absolutely right. Never trust anything but the grace of God in yourself or in anyone else." [3]

OSWALD CHAMBERS

My life-long friend Sherry has lost all sexual interest in her husband, Mike. She stays involved in community efforts, church events, their children's education, and just about every other pursuit imaginable. At one time she warmly welcomed Mike's advances, but after years of his late-night work hours and his indifference to her (except when he wanted sex), Sherry gave up, grew cold, and reasoned *I don't need him anymore.* Mike can't understand why Sherry is so distant. He reasons, "I've worked hard all these years to provide for you and the kids. All I want is a little affection. Why don't you appreciate what I've done for you?" Sherry looks to almost anything for her validation, while Mike looks to Sherry. Both fail to look to God for His approval and affirmation. Both hold fast to their rights and fail to extend the grace that will bring about their healing.

Janna resents Ted's lack of initiative. *What happened to my fearless knight? What happened to his promise to give me a better life? Where did his ambitions go?* Janna publicly chides Ted, believing her criticism will motivate him to find a better job. Attempting to drown out Janna's relentless nagging, Ted turns the volume up on his new surround sound system. He has his own questions. *What happened to my beautiful bride? What happened to my high school sweetheart who cheered me on at every game? Where is the woman whose face lit up when I walked into the room?* Each selfishly holds fast to their rights, refuses to serve, and justifies their feelings. Neither one stops to ask God for His help or infilling.

What do Sherry, Mike, Janna, and Ted share in common? The same thing we all do—a selfish nature that resists surrender.

Regardless of upbringing, socioeconomic status, gender, or race, we all share a selfish nature. Marriage requires us to exchange our selfish nature for Christ's servant-like nature. The truth is, our marriages offer us the clearest revelation of our relationship with Christ. How we treat one another in this closest human relationship reveals the clearest indication of our heart's condition. Why? Because our marriages test us, mold us, and challenge us as no other earthly relationship can. As couples, we need to understand that *surrendering our rights to God is non-negotiable.*

Will surrender be easy? Of course not.

Will it be accomplished in a single moment? Oh, I wish—but no.

However, surrender is essential if we want thriving marriages through every circumstance of life.

So the questions remain: Are you living surrendered? Do you insist on your rights? Or do you awake each morning asking, "Lord, how can I serve You today? And how would You have me demonstrate Your love to my spouse?"

In *The Purpose Driven Life,* Rick Warren writes, "Surrender is not the best way to live; it is the only way to live. Nothing else works. All other approaches lead to frustration, disappointment, and self-destruction... Surrendering your life is not a foolish emotional impulse but a rational, intelligent act, the most responsible and sensible thing you can do with your life."[4]

"One does not surrender a life in an instant. That which is lifelong can only be surrendered in a lifetime."[5]

ELISABETH ELLIOT

No matter how right or justified we feel, if we want greater intimacy in our relationship, we need to surrender our emotions, our beliefs, and our marriage to God. Only as our needs are fully met in Him are we willing or able to embrace marriage as He intended.

Take a moment to reflect on the following questions. As you read, resist thoughts of *I sure hope my spouse reads this. I hope they begin to understand all the ways they need to change.* Instead, consider the areas God might ask *you* to surrender.

① Speaking up/
affirmation
(compliment)
② Faith not sight

Questions to Ask

1. Do I encourage my spouse, or do I focus on what is lacking in our relationship? In *The 7 Habits of Highly Effective People*, the late Stephen R. Covey wrote, "If you want to have a happy marriage, be the kind of person who generates positive energy and sidesteps negative energy."[6] Friend, you cannot control another person, but you do possess the power to control yourself.

2. Do I put my spouse's needs above my own, or do I privately resent all the ways they aren't meeting mine? Charles R. Swindoll writes, "A good marriage isn't so much finding the right partner as it is being the right partner. And that starts with you."[7]

3. Am I holding my spouse responsible for the shortcomings or sins of others, including my own? Sandra Aldrich writes, "We carry into all our new relationships who we are from our previous experiences."[8]

Look, I get it. Changing is tough, and serving is nearly impossible, especially as long as we remain convinced our spouse is to blame!

When God challenged me to surrender, I struggled. *Why should I change when Greg's to blame? He should be the one to change! After all, God, he's the one with all the issues, not me!* Looking back, I laugh and sometimes wonder if God shook His head at my naiveté.

"All a man's ways seem right to him, but the LORD weighs the heart."

PROVERBS 21:2

Until I accepted God's invitation to completely surrender my thoughts, emotions, and needs, I zeroed in on all the areas Greg needed to improve, remaining blind to my faults. I hid behind my pain, pointed at Greg's shortcomings, and wondered why he grew tired of my "support" (nagging) for his betterment.

Accepting God's invitation to surrender my marriage healed it. I began understanding the areas of my life that needed repair, and I gradually experienced the freedom of an identity secured through Christ. I changed from being *needy* to a person who lavished grace, acceptance, and love (at least on *most* days—LOL!).

So, how do you become the type of person who generates happiness rather than negativity? The answer is simple: Surrender all your dreams, needs, ambitions, and feelings to God.

Love is the greatest thing of all,
for love is God-like above everything. [9]

ANDREW MURRAY

True surrender superimposes God's character on our character. Surrender invites God's ability to extend grace. When we surrender and invite God's help, we receive the power to speak words of affirmation and extend love to our spouse unconditionally.

Every sequential step in this book works only under the premise of a surrendered heart. God invites us to partner with Him by providing the keys to life transformation through His Word.

Take a moment to consider the following verses, and reflect on areas God may ask you to surrender. ① Control - fix things ② Logic / Common sense

Verses to Consider Trust/Faith
↓
Emotional healing

1. 1 Peter 5:5 states, "All of you, clothe yourselves with humility toward one another, because, 'God opposes the proud but gives grace to the humble.'" In their book *Moments with You*, Dennis and Barbara Rainey write: "Lives that are being constantly molded and characterized by a fear of the Lord will move toward humility and self-denial rather than living to satisfy self."[10] In our humility, we receive grace. Do you demand your rights? In what ways does God want you to serve instead of expecting to be served? What is the one area you need God to heal in your marriage? Take it to Him in prayer.

2. Hebrews 4:16 encourages us to "approach the throne of grace with confidence, so that we may receive mercy and find grace to help us in our time of need." God invites you to cast your cares on Him. He wants to spend time talking with you. In your marriage, when you address problems, is your first reaction to complain to your spouse or call to God in prayer? Do you try to take control over the situation, or do you ask for God's wisdom and intervention? Do you insist on pointing out your spouse's flaws, or quietly see God's power to transform you and your spouse?

Don't say I told you so, etc...

3. Philippians 2:3-5 states: "Do nothing out of selfish ambition or vain conceit, but in humility consider others better than yourselves. Each of you should look not only to your own interests, but also to the interests of others. Your attitude should be the same as that of Christ Jesus." Wow! That's a tall order! But think about it. What if we truly humbled ourselves and served as Christ served? What do you think would happen if you blessed instead of cursed those who mistreated you? What

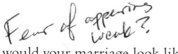

Fear of appearing weak?

would your marriage look like if you chose to live at peace and preferred your spouse's needs over your own?

Our expectations, the taming of our tongue, and showing respect won't occur naturally; they require our intentionality. We must deliberately align our thoughts and our will with God's Word.

> *Don't trust every feeling. Emotions can betray.*
> *Don't justify wrong behavior. Instead, submit every*
> *thought, feeling, and desire to God, and line up*
> *every action and emotion with His Truth.*

Surrender comes in stages. It starts with our conscious decision to submit, and it is followed by our ongoing positive actions. The beautiful part of surrender is the great freedom and healing it delivers.

As I surrendered to God, Greg sensed my effort to change and freely reciprocated his love. As my paradigms shifted, so did Greg's. Check out his perspective:

Greg's Turn

I hope you don't think Julie deserves all the blame for our early chaos! The truth about our crazy, passionate, googly-eyed, love-bird, spitfire, temperamental, knock-down-drag-out, name-calling romance will resonate a bit more realistically with my perspective. Stay tuned . . . I'll take you back a few years.

I remember the first time I saw her. My jaw dropped as she floated by with those big, round shiny blue eyes. (Easy, guys, I said *eyes!*) She was wearing a plaid mid-thigh length skirt and long schoolgirl socks. *Wow!* I thought. *She's hot!* I was mesmerized.

We were both in our late twenties. Julie was my dream come true. She was a good girl. A Christian girl. She was everything I ever wanted. She liked to hold my hand. She laughed at my jokes. She seemed agreeable with just about anything as long as it made me happy and we were together. I wanted to be with her and make her happy.

I immediately broke off my relationship with every other girl-friend. Yes, I was *that kind of guy*, but no matter, Julie's love for me made me feel like a new man. My buddies were not nearly as excited about my newfound love, but eventually even they would realize my bar-hopping, woman-chasing days were over. Julie was the center of my attention now.

Then we got married.

From there, it didn't take long for the explosions to begin. Talk about a paradox. Two people were never more in love; yet at the exact same time, the more we were together, the more we fought. Julie had battle scars from an abusive childhood. She had experienced her share of bad relationships. I understood her need for assurance, but the more she looked for me to give it, the more I resisted. I was an independent cuss—I didn't want to answer to anyone! "Where are you going, and when will you be home?" Julie asked. "Hey! I don't have to answer to you. I'm a grown man, not a child!" I yelled. And there you have it. *Here we go again,* I thought.

On the night she writes about at the beginning of this chapter, I exclaimed, "I can't live like this anymore!" and sped off. For some reason, that didn't go over too well.

It was a difficult season that nearly destroyed our marriage. I felt confined and not about to back away from the line I had drawn in the sand.

Are you beginning to get the picture?

Thankfully, God intervened. Though His answer was available to us both, the transformation began in Julie. Starting with her prayer that late evening, God's love began to penetrate the hard, insensitive shell surrounding my heart. As Julie surrendered *me* to God, I reciprocated. I went out fishing a little less. I looked for opportunities to spend quality time with her. I started offering information about when I would be home—and then showed up early to surprise her. Our marriage took a new path toward healing.

You may want to read that again. I didn't say Julie surrendered to *me.* Thank goodness she didn't; we'd be in a worse mess if that had been the case. No, Julie surrendered herself and me *to Him,* and little by little, we began to feel the love we were trying to hold on to.

One dictionary defines surrender as "to give up in favor of another."[11] That's exactly what Julie did. As she poured her heart out to God that night, she truly surrendered—which changed her response to me. I was stubborn, but over time, my response to her changed as well. Julie surrendered her needs; I surrendered my rights. Julie surrendered her insecurities; I surrendered my attitude. We both surrendered our lives and needs to God, and it was only then that He was allowed to move, as only He can, and repair our broken hearts.

So, how about you? Are you willing to leave your rights at the cross? Will you submit your needs to God even if you feel you already have a thousand times before? Are you willing to surrender your attitude? Are you willing to surrender all you are, and your marriage, into the hands of His Holy Spirit?

Surrender truly supersedes every additional step found in this book. So will you at least suspend your impressions of what is lacking in your relationship? Will you relinquish your pain and trust God to restore your hope? Will you bravely ask God how He wants you to live and love more like Him?

If so, and you truly mean it—then take heart! You are on a wonderful journey, and over time you will experience God's beautiful presence. It won't be easy, but you'll see significant changes as His Spirit equips you to be the spouse He intended.

Keep your heart focused on Christ; after all, as Oswald Chambers wrote, "It takes a heart in love with Jesus Christ to put the feet in His footprints, and to square the life to a steady going 'up to Jerusalem' with Him."[12]

We pray God empowers and equips you as you take up your cross to follow Him in your marriage.

A Letter from the Father

My Dear Child,

Every moment of every day, I see you.[13] When you feel as though you are alone, I am near.[14] Nothing can separate you from My love. I see your struggles. I see your pain. I see how you tirelessly strive to do more, to be better. I see how you run from one activity to the next, hoping, wishing, longing for something to fulfill you. I see your disappointment when your spouse doesn't deliver.[15]

Oh, My precious child, how I long to draw you near to Me, to lift you up, to give you strength. Today, I invite you to hear My voice; don't harden your heart toward Me.[16] Listen closely! You will find what you need. Rest in Me, and you will find strength for your soul.[17] Trust in My love.[18]

When you feel weary, I invite you to cast your cares on Me.[19] Remember who I am. Remember who I have called you to be. Remember what I have promised you. I am the God who grants you the very breath you just breathed![20] I am the God who parts the Red Sea.[21] I am the God who shuts the mouths of lions.[22] I am the God who promises to not withhold anything from the one who loves Me, who is called according to My purpose.[23]

What will you ask of Me?[24] What do you need? Remember, I am good.[25] My love for you endures forever.[26] Just as you desire to give the best to those you love, so do I![27] Surrender your plans, your dreams, your concerns to Me. Surrender your marriage and your spouse; entrust them to Me. Then watch and see what I will do.[28]

With all My love,
Your heavenly Father

Closing Prayer

Father, I admit at times I've felt hurt, broken, and disillusioned. I desperately want to surrender and not pick up any burdens again, but I need Your help. Intervene in my life and my marriage.

Father, I know You are willing to restore; help my unbelief. At times, I feel weary, but You promised You would never leave us or forsake us. Empower me to surrender. Make this marriage better; I release it to You. Equip me to be the spouse You created me to be.

I confess my sins, especially of trying to do things on my own. Lead me by Your Holy Spirit, and I will follow. Be near to me. Let me sense Your direction and give me wisdom. Remind me of the instructions and promises contained in Your Word. Make my marriage thrive.

I pray in Jesus' name. Amen.

A Practical Application

Set aside time to pray specifically for your marriage. As you pray, consider the questions contained within this chapter. Invite God to change in you the areas of your life needing change. Ask Him to help you forgive and remove any wrong attitudes.

You may find it helpful to write out your prayers. Be sure to have your Bible nearby; practice sitting quietly for a few minutes, and invite God to speak to you through His Word.

For Your Reflection

Our marriages offer us the clearest revelation of our relationship with Christ. How we treat one another in this closest human relationship reveals the clearest indication of our heart's condition. Why? Because our marriages test us, mold us, and prepare us as no other earthly relationship can. The key to having an incredible marriage hinges on one key element—our complete surrender to God; a surrender not reliant on our ability or reasoning or even in putting faith in ourselves or our spouse, but a surrender putting our hope and faith in God alone.

God never promised us a problem-free relationship, experiencing total bliss every moment; He promised us He would be with us. He surpasses our finite minds with His infinite grace and accomplishes the impossible, even when the seemingly impossible surrounds our marriage.

A Moment for Preparation

Transformation begins with a decision to forgive, extending unconditional grace, acceptance, and love to the one who did us harm. C. S. Lewis wrote, "To be a Christian means to forgive the inexcusable because God has forgiven the inexcusable in you."[1]

Ask yourself: Do I extend grace easily? Or do I hold on to offenses? Reflect on the idea that God forgives you freely, repeatedly, and unconditionally . . . and then consider: Is there someone to whom God wants me to extend that same kind of grace?

FORGIVE, FREELY

"Get rid of all bitterness, rage and anger, brawling and slander, along with every form of malice. Be kind and compassionate to one another, forgiving each other just as in Christ God forgave you."

EPHESIANS 4:31-32

I met Gina at a conference. Her contagious smile masked years of heartache. From the outside, she appeared to have it altogether. Then, during one of my relationship workshops, Gina broke down as God broke in. Afterward, she bravely shared her testimony with me.

Subsequently, through letters and phone conversations Gina shared details from her life and gave me permission to share them with you. "I grew up in a conservative home with high expectations of strict morality," she said. In other words, don't drink, don't swear, and don't date boys who do. "My dad was the head deacon of our church. I never went to public school or dated until college.

"During my junior year of college, friends and family members pressured me to get my 'MRS. Degree.' I obliged by marrying Daniel the year I graduated."

Gina's life looked picturesque. She appeared to enjoy the white picket fence and greener grass of life. But behind her picture-perfect facade brewed a raging storm. She and Daniel fought constantly. Her marriage quickly unraveled from every corner. Daniel's affair devastated and nearly destroyed what hope she still held.

Despite her pain, Gina fought hard to save her marriage. Externally, for the sake of her children, Gina appeared strong. However, internally Gina was falling apart. Eventually her brokenness sought comfort. She frequented bars and reached out for male companionship.

"I was desperate to feel loved. I gave myself sexually to a lot of men. I guess I wanted to hurt Daniel. But instead, he liked what I was doing and encouraged it! He even set me up with other men. We ended up swinging and going to sex clubs.

"At times, I loved the attention. But honestly, I just wanted my husband to fight for me, to protect me . . . he didn't. I couldn't believe the life I was living."

Gina continued, "As time passed, I met someone and fell in love with him. He promised me a future with financial security. As a wealthy man, he made me feel safe. That's when I got really scared. I knew I was at a crossroads. I needed to make a decision.

"I asked myself, *Can I do this to my kids? What if I'm just trading one problem for a greater one? What if I get into this relationship and don't like it?* So, though I couldn't stand Daniel, I stayed with him. I wondered, should I go back to church, hang in there, or move on? I mean, how do you move on after something like this?"

Gina said, "Because of my fear of what others would say, I stayed with Daniel and broke off the other relationship. I tried my best to forget, my best to forgive, and my best to move forward. But I couldn't!"

Then, at age forty-four, Gina encountered God in a new way. During one of my conference workshops God grabbed hold of her heart through the stories I shared of personal encounters with God's love. God challenged her to forgive Daniel's indiscretions as she heard me talking about my journey of freedom, and He changed her way of thinking. Gina applied His truths and listened for His instructions. Her surrender and willingness to forgive brought her freedom.

Gina made a decision in her own mind that regardless of how things might turn out, she would commit to release Daniel to God and not hold on to any bitterness from the past.

If I could redo parts of my life, I would err on the side of grace, extending forgiveness even when it wasn't sought, loving with purity even when it wasn't returned.

A couple of weeks after the conference, Gina wrote me a letter. "I no longer hold Daniel unforgiven. Your words about 'If God can forgive me, He will help me to extend that same grace and forgiveness to my man' hit home with me. God is empowering me to love my man the way He loves him.

"I've asked God to change my heart and mind. I am learning how to look for all the incredible qualities Daniel possesses instead of trying to control him. I know now that I need to quit trying to be Daniel's Holy Spirit. And for the first time in my life, he is treating me the way I have always dreamed of. I can actually envision growing old with this man and having the kind of marriage God planned for us. I know we still have a lot of work to do, but with God we will make it."

Whew! I was shocked. Not by the specifics of Gina's story, but by her willingness to forgive and love unconditionally.

Gina discovered a universal truth each one of us must embrace. No matter what our past may hold, no matter our current battles, no matter how great or un-great our marriage is, every couple needs to embrace this universal secret if they want to experience the kind of marriage God intended.

A Powerful Truth
Secret #2—Forgive as God forgave you!

Forgiveness is not easy. Sometimes we think we've forgiven—until the issue resurfaces unexpectedly. So, how do we truly forgive? That's the tricky part!

Paul addresses this war in Romans 7:21-25 by writing, "When I want to do good, evil is right there with me. For in my inner being I delight in God's law; but I see another law at work in the members of my body, waging war against the law of my mind and making me a prisoner of the law of sin at work within my members. What a wretched man I am! Who will rescue me from this body of death? Thanks be to God—through Jesus Christ our Lord!"

Paul nails it!

How do we find power to forgive? By self-will? By focusing on a long list of dos and don'ts? By stuffing down and suppressing our feelings, trying to pretend they don't exist? Absolutely not!

Our ability to forgive derives only from an ongoing, intimate relationship with Jesus Christ. Don't miss this vital point. Our *flesh* resists forgiveness. Self-will is not enough. If left to our own efforts, we will fail miserably. We have to know who God says we are. We have to know His purpose and direction for our life. We have to love Him more than we love our comfort or convenience.

Otherwise we'll go back to what makes sense . . . and sometimes forgiveness doesn't make sense. Sometimes it defies reason. Yet, as Christians, God commands it. Thus, only out of our love relationship to Him, the One who deserves our affection and obedience, will we ever find the strength to truly extend forgiveness.

You see, the truth is, I won't forgive someone naturally or easily. Something far greater than self-will or determination must govern my actions, or I will revert to my more natural desires of asserting my rights and protecting my feelings.

Our greater desire to love God and maintain an intimate relationship with Him changes our motives, thoughts, and feelings from the inside out. His love empowers and compels us to love. Because we understand the grace we received, we are better able to extend that grace. We realize areas where we sinned; we learn to stop focusing on human mistakes because we understand who the true enemy is.

Listen, I've experienced huge heartbreaks in my life. So I get it. I've tried to forgive in my own power, only to find all kinds of areas I still needed to release. The only way I learned to extend forgiveness was through my unwavering trust in God. I rest confidently knowing God will protect me. He will defend me. I can trust Him, completely, with everything.

Why? Because He is my Father and He loves me. Like any child who grows up in a loving home and environment, I trust my Father, implicitly. I know He wants the absolute best for me. He has my best interest at heart. He has forgiven me, completely. And, as Jesus said of a woman who had been forgiven from a very sordid past, *the one who's been forgiven much loves much*. I've been forgiven much! I trust God's love. So, when God says to forgive as He forgave me,[2] my love for Him compels me far greater than my desire to defend my rights. When He says if I don't forgive others, He won't forgive me;[3] I don't always understand that, but I trust it. I extend forgiveness graciously because I need gracious forgiveness. I forgive because I know justice belongs to God. I don't wish for vengeance on my enemies . . . because honestly, I know just how much I deserved God's vengeance. Yet, I know God is my avenger, and He can avenge with justice more powerfully than I could ever imagine.

As believers, God's power lives in us, and the more we invite God's Spirit to move freely in our life through intentional steps of obedience to know Him more, the more we become like Him. As we spend time in His presence, His nature becomes our nature and affects our desires and actions.

Isn't that a relief?

Seriously, we don't forgive out of obligation; God actually changes our nature to be like His. It's not us doing it; it is Christ in us. His sustaining love compels and motivates our forgiveness, overtaking every other fleshly desire raging against us.

When Greg and I wed, we pledged traditional wedding vows. We promised to love one another, cherish one another, forsake all others, and live committed to one another for better or for worse, for richer or for poorer, in sickness and in health, until death do us part.

Whew! Let the enormity of those vows soak in! As you can imagine, it didn't take long for our vows to be tested. It didn't take long to identify the unwritten conditions I'd placed on those vows.

"God intended the marriage relationship to be a reflection of His relationship to us—a relationship that remains steadfast because it isn't based on fickle feelings or human worthiness but rather is based on uncompromising commitment."[4]

SHANNON ETHRIDGE

Oh, I loved Greg, wholeheartedly—as long as he treated me like a princess. I honored and respected him selflessly—as long as he extended honor to me. I remained committed to him, for better or worse—as long as his priorities matched all of mine. Unfortunately, I justified each condition . . . until God challenged me to honor each vow unconditionally.

It's important to note, as we live and join together with our spouses, that even the most perfect spouse makes mistakes. Even a well-intending spouse overlooks needs.

Rob gives his job and hobbies precedence over Jenni's needs. Maranda feels rejected by Russell's indifference to her and frustrated by his lack of involvement with their children. John rarely extends Maggie a kind word or offers a simple thank-you for the ways she serves him. Then there's Ariel, who continues to disregard her appearance; she's indifferent to Alan, who shares, "I don't expect her to be a supermodel, but a little make-up or styling of her hair would communicate that she still respects me." Teresa is so critical of Jeff that he no longer attempts to do anything around the house because he knows Teresa will tell him he's not doing it "right." Each couple privately holds on to their offense. Their bitterness creates physical, emotional, and spiritual distance.

Conflicts are inevitable regardless of the offense— because of the intimate nature shared between a husband and a wife. The question isn't if we will need to forgive but whether we will forgive.

Releasing offenses isn't found by analyzing whether we are right or wrong, or whether our expectations are realistic or godly.

The key to releasing our offense occurs by placing our allegiance in God and focusing our attention on His instruction.

Questions to Ask

1. Do I seethe with anger when I reflect on my spouse's past wrongs? Do I snarl in disgust when I think of the way he/she disappoints me? Do I attack my spouse on little issues because I am secretly fuming over a much bigger injustice done to me? Neil T. Anderson writes, "You don't forgive someone merely for their sake; you do it for your sake so you can be free. Your need to forgive isn't an issue between you and the offender; it's between you and God. Forgiveness is agreeing to live with the consequences of another person's sin. Forgiveness is costly; we pay the price of the evil we forgive. Yet you're going to live with those consequences whether you want to or not; your only choice is whether you will do so in the bitterness of unforgiveness or the freedom of forgiveness."[5]

2. Am I willing to forgive? Do I harbor and hold on to the painful memories from my past and the wrongs I feel I've encountered? Are there ways I need to forgive and allow God to heal my pain? In her book *The Power of a Praying Wife*, Stormie Omartian writes, "While no one can pretend the past didn't happen, it's possible to pray that all the effects of it are removed. No one is destined to live with them forever."[6]

3. What consumes my thinking? Do I extend grace and believe the best about my spouse? Do I focus on things that irritate me about them? How can I foster a greater trust, friendship, and love within my marriage? In *What I Wish My Mother Had Told Me About Men*, I shared the principle, "We gravitate toward what we contemplate."[7] What is your focus? Do you dwell on your spouse's best qualities or their worst?

When you harbor and hold on to the painful memories of your past or the wrongs you feel you've encountered, you paralyze yourself from moving forward. Further, you empower the offender to manipulate your decisions, your peace, and your life's fulfillment.

At one time, forgiveness of what happened during my childhood seemed impossible to me. Oh, I said I forgave, but then lived with the weight of needing to protect myself from harm. I thought I had dealt with those issues. I thought I had released my perpetrators. I thought I'd forgiven all the men who had abused me or broken my trust—but I had not!

My pain tasked Greg with an uphill climb. My brokenness demanded his perfection. I allowed no room for error. Inevitably, as all humans do, Greg made mistakes. I exaggerated his imperfections, magnifying them by the sins of countless others. Consumed with skepticism, fear, and unforgiveness, I sometimes disregarded Greg's thoughtfulness and scrutinized his gestures. I wondered, *Is he being sincere? What's his motive? What's he trying to hide?*

Early in the first year of our marriage, Greg surprised me with a romantic weekend getaway. Instead of recognizing his effort to communicate his love, I remained rigid the entire weekend, convinced he planned the date only out of guilt because the weekend before he'd left me with the kids and gone on an all-night fishing outing with his buddies.

Pathetic, I know! I mean, can you imagine living with someone who didn't trust or believe anything positive about you?

How about you? Do you ever struggle to believe the best about your spouse? Have past wrongs left you skeptical, cynical? Was your childhood similar to mine, where every abuse was present? If so, here is some good news from my friend Sandra Aldrich: "Childhood experiences affect marriages, but no one has to be controlled by them." [8]

> *"The past should not be a place where we live,*
> *but something from which we learn."* [9]
>
> STORMIE OMARTIAN

For me, forgiveness occurred in stages and was only made possible as I encountered a greater revelation of God's love for me. His affirmation and affection made me less inclined to protect myself. Understanding God's protection enabled me to release the damage other people had inflicted upon my life. Knowing God truly loved me and passionately defended me, freed me to love without reservation. I embraced more fully who God is and who He says I am, which empowered me to love without fear.

In their book *Relationships*, Drs. Les and Leslie Parrott (husband and wife) share, "If you try to find intimacy with another person before achieving a sense of identity on your own, all your relationships become an attempt to complete yourself." [10]

When we accept God's unconditional love and allow Him to define our worth, He equips us to extend that love to others. When we pursue God passionately and saturate our thoughts with His Word, He provides hope and healing.

Verses to Consider

1. Jesus, while hanging on the cross, prayed, "Father, forgive them, for they do not know what they are doing."[11] He offered this prayer from the abundance found in His relationship to the Father. Jesus knew who God the Father said He was. He knew His mission and didn't live for temporal gratification.

How does Jesus' selflessness inspire you to forgive? What changes do you need to make to be able to respond that freely? Do you realize (as a believer) that the same Spirit that raised Christ from the dead lives in you, empowering you to live as Jesus lived?

2. Mathew 18:18 states, "I tell you the truth, whatever you bind on earth will be bound in heaven, and whatever you loose on earth will be loosed in heaven." If you hold on to offenses and fail to extend forgiveness, you bind that sin and offense to your heart and become paralyzed in its grip.

In order for bitterness to be released, acknowledge that it exists. Don't oversimplify and just quickly say, "I forgive you." Forgiveness must be genuine. Have you ever flippantly said, "I forgive you," but then muttered judgment under your breath? Have you ever tried to will away your feelings or live in denial of them, only to find them resurfacing? Are there areas of anger, hatred, or discontentment you need to confess so God can heal you?

3. James 5:16 says, "Therefore confess your sins to each other and pray for each other so that you may be healed. The prayer of a righteous man is powerful and effective." Gaining godly wisdom and accountability is essential for healing. Prayers of righteous men and women provide accountability and

encouragement to areas where we may be weak. Are you bottled up, busy playing the perfect couple? Do you pretend you have it all together? Is there a godly couple you can go to for prayer and accountability?

Remember, forgiving doesn't mean you blindly ignore issues. But neither should you address every issue presenting itself; choose to focus on what really matters. Work toward a middle ground of understanding, compassion, and mercy.

How?

By expressing value in your spouse, asking clarifying questions to understand their needs, and then committing to work on meeting their need. Promote intimacy by saying, "I really want you to know how much I love and respect you. How you feel is important to me. Can you share a simple way I can meet this need and demonstrate my commitment to you?"

"Forgiveness is the Divine miracle of grace." [12]

OSWALD CHAMBERS

Ideally, both you and your spouse will commit to this process. But even if they don't, you can still do what is right.

Releasing bitterness and extending forgiveness demands a lot of concentrated effort. But in the end we will reap the rewards of a fuller and more joyful life. I know Greg and I sure have!

Greg's Turn

I've heard it said that harboring bitterness is like drinking poison and waiting for the other person to die. Isn't that true? If I refuse to forgive Julie for something she's done, it harms me far more than it harms her. Once I accepted that truth, I took the first step toward making positive changes.

My journey of healing was slightly different than Julie's. Our issues were different. Because of past abuse and betrayal by others, Julie was suspicious and felt the need to control. My bitterness was fed by my own anger that I was the one who had to clean up the mess in Julie's life that others had created! I felt justified being angry and bitter towards her. After all, she was the one who pressed my buttons. From my view, her incessant questions and cross-examinations were the problem, not my temper or flirtatious personality.

After months of fighting, I soon realized that our marriage was doomed if I continued to hold that attitude. In truth, we both needed a lot of healing. Julie made the first move by seeking God. It took time for her to practice what she heard from Him, but she was clearly trying to change some of her negative behaviors and thought patterns. Now it was my turn.

"I'm going fishing," I said one day as I prepared my tackle. I braced for Julie's response. She was about to start the drill: "What time will you be home?" "Where are you fishing?" "Who's going with you?" It really wasn't her questions that bothered me, it was the sleuthy tone. I knew we were about to have a conversation that could have no good outcome. I waited as I mentally prepared my answers: *I'm fishing on Table Rock Lake. No one is going with me, and I don't know when I'll be home. I'm just going fishing!* I waited . . .

To my surprise, her response was not a question at all. "Well, have fun and catch a big one!" she said. "See you when you get back."

Relieved, I kissed her, loaded up the boat, and headed to the lake.

As I pursued the illustrious bass ("ol' slobber lips," as my pastor affectionately named him), I couldn't help but think of Julie's face. I missed her. Before, I had generally fished until I *had* to come home. Today I wanted to get home early.

And so began the healing.

Obviously we still had a lot of work to do, but from that point forward I can honestly say our relationship changed. We still had our "moments," and truthfully we still do, but I've learned from her example. As Julie restrained her natural tendency to indulge in detective questioning, I was able to respond to her needs more readily. Over time, I was able to let go of my own bitterness and embrace her, even in her weaker moments.

A Letter from the Father

My Child,

Cry out to Me. Tell Me your pain, and know this: I care for you.[13]
I have grafted you into My family, and your cries come before My very throne.[14] *Release your offenses, that you might know the joy of forgiveness and experience the hope found only in Me. Forgive as I forgave you.*[15]

You are safe with Me.[16] *Others will disappoint, but I will not!*[17] *If you will turn to Me, you will discover a love that removes the pain you once thought unbearable. The offenses that seemed unimaginable to forgive will vanish in light of the surpassing revelation of My love for you.*[18] *Though you suffered for a little while, you will find hope and healing in My Presence.*[19]

My perfect love casts out fear.[20] *Every trial, every offense, when yielded to Me, bears life.*[21] *I will take what the enemy intended for evil and use it to reveal the depths and power of My love for you.*[22]

But I require your surrender.[23] *Trust Me. Draw near to Me, and I will draw near to you.*[24] *I will create new life in you, and you will be remade.*[25] *You can't "will" surrender into existence. Surrender isn't birthed by ambition. Instead, it is a gift I gladly extend to you.*[26] *Allow Me to be your Defender. Embrace My love for you, and the offenses of others won't embitter you.*[27] *When you are persecuted, you share in the sufferings of My Son and thus will share in His glory.*[28] *When you extend forgiveness, you will more fully understand the depths of My love for you.*

And know this: I have loved you with an everlasting love. My love will sustain you and empower you to forgive.[29]

Closing Prayer

Father, I choose right now to release all the pain from my past. Help me to forgive and release my offenders. I desperately want to be free from negative memories.

I know harboring bitterness is not pleasing to You. Forgive me for trying to forgive in my own effort. Forgive me for trying to protect myself. I know You are my Defender. So protect me, Lord, from those who would intentionally harm me. Defend me. Help me to live in complete freedom and to love with all of my heart.

Help me especially to show love and respect to my spouse. I release all of my "rights" and submit them to You. Change me and give me the strength to love, as You love, unconditionally.

Father, I know You are willing to answer this prayer. You said if we ask anything in accordance with Your Word, You would hear us and we would have whatever we asked for. So, thank You for helping me to forgive. I release every broken dream and painful memory. Erase every offense from my thoughts; help me never to ponder them again or use them as ammunition against my spouse. Make my marriage thrive.

I pray, in Jesus' name. Amen.

For Your Reflection

Because of the intimate relationship shared between a husband and a wife, conflicts are inevitable. Be quick to forgive, slow to become angry, and allow God to infuse you with His unconditional love. The same grace leading you to repentance will assist you to extend forgiveness. You are not alone!

As you surrender your marriage to God and forgive your spouse, God will heal your marriage. Forgive as God forgave you. Remember, no matter the offense incurred, if you fail to forgive, you will suffer physically, emotionally, and spiritually.

A Practical Application

At the age of four, my nephew Aaron experienced severe burns. While in the intensive care unit, nurses scrubbed his feet purposely to tear off old skin and allow new skin to form and heal correctly. The process was excruciating, but necessary. If left unattended, Aaron's infection would have spread through his bloodstream and proved fatal.

No one wanted Aaron to suffer, but the cleansing process and the peeling back of damaged skin was necessary. Likewise, the Holy Spirit scrubs over our life again and again in order to peel away infectious thinking. At times, the removal of impurities is extremely painful, but the process is necessary. "Development" "IfTests"

How is the Holy Spirit brushing across your wounds? What impurities does He want to remove from your life? Spend time inviting the Lord to reveal any area needing to be surrendered to Him. Ask for His help to extend forgiveness.

For greater growth, reflect on the "Questions to Ask" and "Verses to Consider" sections provided in this chapter.

A Moment for Preparation

*Transformation grows with our decision to believe the best about
another, remembering their best qualities, and overlooking their offenses.
Tammy Maltby writes, "See in all things, in everything, a chance to die to
self and the pride that comes from defending yourself and your rights."* [1]

*Are there ways you shift the blame in your relationship? Do you excuse
or fail to acknowledge your areas of responsibility? Do you tend to
believe the best about your spouse, or do you gravitate toward
negativity and finger-pointing? Do your actions foster grace and
mercy or more of a get-even mentality?*

DON'T SHIFT
THE BLAME

*"Do not judge, and you will not be judged. Do not condemn,
and you will not be condemned. Forgive, and you will be forgiven.
Give, and it will be given to you. A good measure, pressed down,
shaken together and running over, will be poured into your lap.
For with the measure you use, it will be measured to you."*

LUKE 6:37-38

For the first two years of our marriage, Greg and I insisted on our rights and instigated blame on the other.

Unbelievable! I fumed. *I can't believe he's going fishing again! This is the fourth time this week!* I clenched my teeth trying to restrain my frustrations.

Immediately another part of my brain responded, *C'mon, Julie, be positive. Greg works hard. He needs a break. Quit being so critical!*

I meditated on God's Word and tried to convince myself not to be angry. I wanted to support Greg's dreams, but couldn't stop the ensuing rage mounting in my heart as I watched him pack his fishing gear. I hated his stupid boat! I wanted to bash a hammer against its shiny metallic finish.

Then my thoughts shifted. *Really? It's ten below zero, and you're going fishing? How about going to a movie with me? A date night? Heck, I'd settle for mac and cheese out of a box and a night in if you'd simply stay home with me.*

When Greg and I first married, he aspired to become a professional fisherman. He literally fished four to five times a week during hot seasons of the year and a minimum of three times in midwinter—yep, even when it was ten below zero.

From my perspective, we needed to spend quality time together. Our children needed a normal family life. Professional fishing didn't provide that. In order to participate in fishing tournaments, Greg needed to travel frequently.

I didn't like being left alone. Being left alone equated to not being loved.

Quite simply, Greg's plans conflicted with mine. As a new mother, I longed for Greg's help. For three years straight, our first-born, Sommer, awakened several times a night. I averaged only four hours of sleep. And, I worked full-time.

Between sleepless nights, work, cooking, cleaning and all the challenges of being a new mommy and step-mommy, I needed *down* time. These were real, felt needs. Why couldn't Greg run to my rescue? Why didn't he understand life from my perspective? Why did a stupid worm and hook hold more meaning to him than me?

Whoa! Hold the show! By now you may be thinking, I'd be ticked off too. But what you wouldn't know is all the times Greg did stay home and all the times he did take me to the movies. From his perspective he could never win. Many times when he did

"Too good to be true"

express his love, I couldn't receive it because of my colored past. I viewed his gestures through skeptical eyes and often questioned his motives.

From his perspective, I was unreasonable. He saw my actions as clingy, selfish, and self-centered. From his perspective, he demonstrated love to me every day by working long hours. He bore the financial burdens for our family and shouldered extensive responsibility at work. The demands of his job weighed heavy. As much as I need down time, so did he; fishing provided him with a peaceful outlet that he desperately needed. *Why can't you let me be a man? Why do you always have to nag? Why won't you let me relax and get refueled?*

Enough never seemed enough for either of us.

"You never let me just be a guy . . . I don't know what you want from me!" Greg exclaimed. "I can't sit around gazing into your eyes twenty-four hours a day. You're clingy. You're smothering me!"

I retaliated. "All I want is for you to want to be here with me. Why can't you help? I need your help. I wouldn't be so clingy if you'd help me out."

Ding-ding. The bell rang, and once again we bounced up from our individual corners, stood toe-to-toe and nose-to-nose, ready to fight. Selfishness and self-centeredness stood ready to duke it out. We jabbed one verbal punch of accusation and followed it with another blow of shifting the blame.

Who won? No one!

Well, actually there was a winner, someone we cluelessly overlooked. Maybe you've overlooked him too. He's sneaky. He's crafty. And he loves causing dissension. As Greg and I blamed one another, Satan relished in his victory. The Bible clearly states that the devil desires to steal, to kill, and to destroy.[2] Early in our marriage, Greg and I failed to recognize the enemy's tactic of shifting the blame, a tactic originating in the Garden of Eden.

"The search for a scapegoat is the easiest of all hunting expeditions."[3]

PRESIDENT DWIGHT D. EISENHOWER

Genesis 3:9-19 records the first episode of shifting the blame. You know the story: God asked Adam, "Where are you?" and he replied, "I hid because I was naked." God said, "Who told you that you were naked? Have you eaten from the tree that I commanded you not to eat from?" And Adam said, "The woman you put here with me—she gave me some fruit from the tree, and I ate it."

There it is—the first shift of blame. Adam could have said, "Yep, I did it." But instead he pointed to Eve. *It was her fault, God.* As soon as the Lord turned to the woman, she said, "The serpent deceived me, and I ate." There it is—the second shift of blame. Again, no one wanted to stand up to take accountability.

Oh, how little has changed.

Finally, God addressed Satan directly, not asking any questions, knowing that ultimately Satan had started it all. Genesis 3:14 relates, "Because you have done this, Cursed are you above all the livestock and all the wild animals! You will crawl on your belly and you will eat dust all the days of your life. And I will put enmity between you and the woman, and between your offspring and hers; he will crush your head, and you will strike his heel."

God instantly acknowledged a truth every couple must embrace. Our true enemy is not one another; our true enemy is the master deceiver warned about in 1 Peter 5:8. "Be self-controlled and alert. Your enemy the devil prowls around like a roaring lion looking for someone to devour." The enemy looks for any opportunity to destroy marriage.

One way we participate with him is by shifting the blame. If we want our marriages to thrive, we must embrace the following truth.

A Powerful Truth

Secret #3—Don't shift the blame; take responsibility for your own actions.

Reality is a funny thing, because everyone looks at life through their own perspective. Faulty information and our fallen nature skew our perceptions. Taking responsibility for our own actions, on the other hand, pleases God and invites His restoration into our relationships.

Accountability means I change the way I think. Instead of thinking about what my spouse did wrong, I focus only on my actions. What did I do that caused offense? When I discern my area of responsibility, I acknowledge my actions first before God, and then with my spouse. I finish with the words, "I'm sorry for my part in this; will you please forgive me?"

Being accountable for my actions also means I change what I say. Instead of throwing out sentences beginning with "You" and adding an accusation, I begin by saying "I" and add a confession.

Playing the game of "he did, she did" is dangerous. Nothing ever resolves. Everyone remains embittered.

Roger says, "I wouldn't yell at Kim if she would stop talking to her sister so much and pay attention to what needs to be done around the house." Andrea declares, "I wouldn't act so cold if Tom communicated half as much with me when the lights are on as he does when the lights go out!" Tina hangs her head, "I would have never had the affair if Paul would have paid more attention to me instead of his work." Paul retaliates, "I wouldn't work such long hours if you stopped piling up such huge credit card debt."

Behind each declaration resides a list of unmet needs, disappointments, and underlying thoughts filled with justifications. I understand *justification* all too well. In the early years of our marriage, Greg and I constantly shifted the blame—a practice that nearly destroyed our relationship.

Me: "I wouldn't complain so much if you simply stayed home with me or helped with the kids!"

Greg: "I'd stay home with you more if you wouldn't smother me so much!"

The blame game lasted for hours. At times, we literally fought, physically wrestling with one another, trying to solidify our points of view. Our marriage headed fast and furious toward a bottomless pit. We needed to make changes, quick!

> *"Any fool can criticize, complain, and condemn—*
> *and most fools do. But it takes character and*
> *self-control to be understanding and forgiving."*[4]
>
> DALE CARNEGIE

At some point every marriage faces a crossroads that will dictate its outcome. Andy Stanley has written: "Direction, not intention, determines your destination."[5] One road is filled with selfishness and shouts: "Serve me!" "I deserve . . ." Or, "My needs are more important." The other road is filled with service that's characterized by whispers of "I will serve you." "You deserve to be loved and respected." And, "Your needs are more important than my own."

When faced with such a crossroads in our marriage, I determined to choose the road of service. I'd like to say I chose this road because I was noble or righteous but . . . honestly, I chose it because I was desperate. I knew something needed to change in my marriage, or Greg and I weren't going to survive. Thus, in sheer exhaustion, I asked God to change my heart where it needed to be changed.

The results of my prayer were incredible. God taught me to quit asking, "Where are you going? When will you be home? How long will you be gone this time?" Instead, I began sincerely extending blessings of, "Have a great time. I'll be waiting up for a little more fun (wink, wink) when you get home." Suddenly, Greg became more eager to return home. God seasoned my heart with compassion. He literally changed my desires. I actually wanted to support Greg's needs over my own.

Get this! I genuinely wanted Greg to get rest and have fun more than my own needs. Was I still tired? Yes! Exhausted! But supernaturally, God changed me. Knowing how tired I was compelled my compassion for Greg's fatigue. Friend, only God can do that. (Trust me, I wasn't that gracious.)

Over time, Greg sensed that I accepted his love instead of scrutinizing his every gesture. Oh, he still enjoyed his time away, but he looked forward to coming home to a welcoming wife, rather than a bitter, nagging, ill-tempered one. He appreciated not being bashed by my guilt sessions. He rejoiced when I encouraged him to enjoy his time, and, in return, he became more sensitive to my needs.

He started examining his actions. He began doing nice things for me, like drawing a warm bubble bath and then taking care of our children while I soaked. Occasionally, when the kids were sleeping too, he'd sneak in and wash my hair. Truly romantic!

Other times, he gave me thoughtful gifts. One of my favorites was a beautiful pen and a five-subject notebook. "Take a little extra time for yourself so you can journal. I'll watch the kids for the next couple of hours." Wowza! As a woman who loves to write, it was the perfect gift.

I stood amazed as God did what He had promised me. He healed my brokenness and performed a few changes in my husband, too.

Therefore, in every situation we have a choice. Choosing to believe the best in one another and looking for the opportunities to extend grace causes God's character to grow within us.

Are you getting it? Do you see how change occurs? Shifting the blame may be our natural inclination, but it never solves our conflicts. Pointing fingers at one another proves futile. Justifying why we are right and our spouse is wrong profits nothing. In the end, God sees through our excuses and holds us responsible for our own actions.

So, let's take a moment to examine our hearts and allow God to reveal any areas where we might become a better spouse.

Questions to Ask

1. How might you support more and accuse less? How can you better serve your spouse? How can you better express your love and devotion to your spouse? Charles Swindoll writes, "You see, a wife is not responsible for her husband's life. She is responsible for her life. You cannot make your husband something he is not. Only God can do that . . . Ruth Graham . . . once said, 'It is my job to love Billy. It is God's job to make him good.'"[6]

   [handwritten: Rus leit lol, run both affirmation "I Love you"]

2. Do you notice all of your spouse's flaws while excusing your own? Do you blame your spouse when things go wrong rather than taking responsibility for your actions? If so, ask God to show you how you need to change. Ask Him for specific wisdom to know what you need to do—and then do it.

God never tells us to do anything contrary to His Word. If you don't hear His directions, continue reading the Bible and ask again. Remember, as Ralph Waldo Emerson said, "Every man is entitled to be valued by his best moments."

3. Since our reality is a matter of perspective, ask God to change yours to see your spouse as He sees them. Invite His grace to fill you and to empower you to understand your spouse's perspective. Ask: "What reoccurring conflict consistently appears within my marriage? Do my childhood experiences contribute to these marital conflicts? What do these issues look like from my spouse's perspective?"

   [handwritten: Affection - yes in terms of dating etc...]

In his book *Humility*, the great South African devotional writer Andrew Murray stated: "Humility is not so much a virtue along with the others, but is the root of all, because it alone takes the right attitude before God and allows Him, as God, to do all."[7]

It doesn't matter; whether you are right or wrong, shifting the blame proves futile. But how do you stop justifying your actions or pointing blame at your spouse? Now that's the real question! Scripture addresses it. Here are specific instructions from God's Word that help us to avoid shifting the blame.

Verses to Consider

1. Matthew 5:25-26 encourages us to "settle matters quickly with your adversary who is taking you to court. Do it while you are still with him on the way, or he may hand you over to the judge, and the judge may hand you over to the officer, and you may be thrown into prison. I tell you the truth, you will not get out until you have paid the last penny."

Do you attempt to reach a middle ground of understanding, or do you attempt to determine who's right and who's wrong? Always examine a conflict and your actions by asking, "Did I do everything possible to be a good spouse in this situation?"

2. James 4:1-2 says, "What causes fights and quarrels among you? Don't they come from your desires that battle within you? You want something but don't get it. You kill and covet, but you cannot have what you want. You quarrel and fight. You do not have, because you do not ask God."

Do you point out your spouse's faults? Do you try to manipulate *Yes in situations* him (or her) to think and feel the same as you? *sometimes* I know I sure did. I had to get honest by asking myself, "How's that working for you?"

3. James 1:19-20 says, "My dear brothers, take note of this: Everyone should be quick to listen, slow to speak and slow to become

angry, for man's anger does not bring about the righteous life that God desires."

Do you feel like you need to be God's mouthpiece? Do you speak more than you listen? Do you seek to understand or seek more to be understood?

4. Isaiah 55:1-3 says, "Come, all you who are thirsty, come to the waters; and you who have no money, come, buy and eat! Come, buy wine and milk without money and without cost. Why spend money on what is not bread, and your labor on what does not satisfy? Listen, listen to me, and eat what is good, and your soul will delight in the richest of fare. Give ear and come to me; hear me, that your soul may live."

Who do you seek to satisfy your needs? God hardwired us for relationship, but loving God's creation (our spouse) is different than worshiping His creation (our spouse.) Do you try to demand that your spouse meet all of your needs, or do you press in to God to allow Him to define who you are? Oswald Chambers wrote, "No love of the human heart is safe unless it has been satisfied by God first."[8] God is the only one who will never let us down.

5. First Thessalonians 5:16-18 says, "Be joyful always; pray continually; give thanks in all circumstances, for this is God's will for you in Christ Jesus."

Do you pray more than you complain? Who do you turn to when you are frustrated? Will you entrust your spouse to God and ask Him to reveal what needs to be changed in you, meanwhile letting him address what your spouse needs to change? *Starting to slowly but surely*

WHAT I WISH MY MOTHER HAD TOLD ME ABOUT MARRIAGE

Taking responsibility for our own actions pleases God and invites His restoration into our relationships. He liberates, heals, and delivers the repentant heart. Reprogramming our actions won't be easy, but God is bigger than our habits, and by His grace we can embrace the kind of marriage He intended for us.

He radically changed the way I thought and acted, healing my marriage. As God changed me, He also changed Greg.

Greg's Turn

"What on earth is your problem?"

Julie, remaining rigid in posture, replied with the usual "Nothing."

My voice escalated. "Julie, I can't do this. I don't know how to please you! I'm not going to play this crazy game anymore!" From there I worked myself into a froth of name-calling and pushed her.

Imagine that. A man who had vowed before God, friends, and family to love, honor, and cherish . . . now screaming obscenities at the top of his lungs. Imagine for a moment a man responding to his wife's plea for security with a violent explosion of anger. It was easy to understand Julie's need for affirmation and comfort; I was simply tired of her needing it. At the time, I justified my actions and shifted the blame because her relentless cross-examinations and inability to receive my love pushed me over the edge. I didn't even know who I was anymore.

She was hurting. She felt insecure, afraid. She needed assurance of my love. She needed me to respond with compassion. I blew it! Even today as I recall the moment, it causes me to well up.

What kind of man does that? I'm supposed to be the safest place on earth for her, a refuge where all her cares and insecurities can be revealed without judgment. I'm supposed to protect her, not

— 64 —

GREG AND JULIE GORMAN

find fault, let alone blame her for my own issues. I am her husband. As Paul said to the church of Ephesus, "Husbands, love your wives, just as Christ loved the church and gave himself up for her."[9] To the church in Colossae, Paul instructed, "Husbands love your wives, and do not be harsh with them."[10] When I read those verses, I knew I had failed. Miserably!

I tried to love Julie. I tried to be what she needed, but it wasn't working. In the process, I became embittered toward her, slowly destroying our relationship. We needed help.

Have you ever heard someone making excuses? Have you ever listened as they explained how "I wouldn't if she hadn't . . ." or "It's not my fault, he's the one who . . ."? Have you ever found this attractive? Certainly not. One of the greatest attitudes a person can possess is accountability.

As Julie points out, shifting the blame originated in the Garden of Eden. The inherent problem is that we fail to grow when we insist that all our problems are someone else's fault. Nothing ever improves until we focus on the areas we need to improve within ourselves. As the bumper sticker says, "Be the change you wish to see in the world." There's definite truth in the statement. To grow, we need to look within.

Whose actions do I control? Mine.

Who will answer for my actions? That's right, me!

The point is simple; I can't change anyone except myself. I gain absolutely nothing by shifting the blame. It's not even attractive.

Several years back I mentored a young man who constantly showed up late (among many other issues). I knew I needed to have a tough conversation with him. After thinking about it, I presented this thought. "Travis, from now on, every time you feel the need to explain why something went wrong, I want you to ask yourself this question: What could I have done that may have made a difference in the outcome?"

The phraseology was very specific. I challenged him to ask himself what he *could* have done that *may* have made a difference? The emphasis centered on *could* and *may*. We don't always know how our actions impact our outcome, but when we phrase the question this way, it allows us to look at possibilities. I like considering possibilities. I believe there is much to be gained from it.

For Travis, it proved life-changing. The next time he was late, he had his action step. Rather than blaming the stoplight, or the train, or the wreck on the way in, Travis took responsibility by saying, "I *could* have left my house fifteen minutes earlier, and I *may* have been on time." Thereafter, he began to grow.

I challenge you to watch for ways you shift the blame. When you bust yourself, don't beat yourself up; just stop and ask, what *could* I have done that *may* have made a difference? Be careful to look within yourself for resolution, not at your spouse.

A Letter from the Father

Dear Child,

Everything around you shouts "Defend yourself. Take care of your needs. Get even!" But listen closely, and I will teach you a more excellent way. Love your enemies.[11] Pray for those who do you harm.[12] Do good things for those who hate you or mistreat you.[13] Forgive as I forgave you.[14] Love as I have loved you.[15]

When you feel as though you have been misjudged, remember My love for you; remember how I never retaliated or paid back offense for offense. Instead, I endured to bring about your salvation. Like a lamb to slaughter, I remained silent. My sacrifice brought your salvation.[16]

One day, every person will give an account for their actions and words.[17] Humble yourself now.[18] Take responsibility for your own actions. Confess your sins, so that you might be healed.[19] And then, love as I have loved you. Reveal My love and prove to be My child.[20] Your kind words will turn away anger.[21]

But more importantly, know this: You are not alone.[22] I will not leave you abandoned.[23] I will rise to your cause and defend you.[24] Bear My character and demonstrate My love, and you will witness My deliverance.[25] I will not disappoint you.[26] I will rescue you, for I delight in humility and give grace in time of need.[27]

Closing Prayer

Father, help me to take responsibility for my own actions and not shift the blame to my spouse. In every situation show me how I can be pleasing to You. Equip me to bridle my thoughts and emotions and submit them to You. Help me live according to Your Word.

My tendency is to shift blame and to find fault with my spouse, but I know that isn't from You. Show me through Your Word and the power of Your Holy Spirit how and what I need to surrender. I submit my will to You and want to be pleasing in Your sight.

Forgive me for being judgmental. Help me to be all You ask, and help my spouse be all You desire. I give You every thought, feeling, and emotion. Create in me a pure heart. Cause me to walk righteously and with a loving, gentle spirit. Make our marriage thrive.

I pray in Jesus' name. Amen.

For Your Reflection

Faulty information and our fallen nature skew our perceptions. Therefore, in marriage we have a choice: We can believe the best about our spouse, or we can point out their flaws. Take responsibility for your own actions. Don't shift the blame.

A Practical Application

Indeed, Satan was guilty of arousing temptation, but God still held Adam and Eve accountable individually for their actions. Typically the origins of our fears or weaknesses lie in attempting to gratify our own "needs." We fail to submit to one another because of our self-preserving pride.

Analyze your relationship. Do you attempt to gratify your needs through manipulation? Do you fail to serve your spouse in an attempt to protect yourself? Are you concerned for your spouse's spiritual condition or simply trying to manipulate them to be what you want them to be? Answering these questions transparently proves difficult, but when we confess our hidden attitudes we experience incredible freedom.

Instead of trying to persuade your spouse to be or to do what you want, extend love. Serve. Encourage them to follow their dreams. Let your needs be met in Christ; otherwise your desire will influence your actions. Today, think of one admirable quality you appreciate about your spouse. On a sticky note, write: *One of the things I respect about you the most is . . .* and then post it in a place where your spouse is sure to find it.

One of the . . .

Seeing the best in other ppl + giving them another chance. (B.c I ~~might~~ ~~probably~~ might not have if in your shoes)

A Moment for Preparation

Transformation flourishes when we acknowledge we live in the midst of a spiritual battle. Second Corinthians 4:18 says, "So we fix our eyes not on what is seen, but on what is unseen. For what is seen is temporary, but what is unseen is eternal." Ask God to open your spiritual eyes so you can see the things of the unseen world, where the secrets of eternity are discovered, in such a way you can apply them positively to your marriage.

Do not be deceived. God's arch-enemy seeks to destroy your marriage; do not be naïve to his trickery. The French poet Charles Baudelaire was quoted as saying, "The greatest trick the devil ever pulled was convincing the world he doesn't exist."[1] Ask yourself, Who does God say my true enemy is? Who and what shapes my thoughts? Have I bought in to the enemy's lies?

RESIST THE DEVIL'S LIES

"The devil . . . is a liar and the father of lies."

JOHN 8:44

"How can God forgive us so easily?" my daughter, Sommer, asked. "I mean, we don't deserve it!" She held her breath and tightened her lips, as if by doing so she might possibly hold back the tears forming in the corners of her eyes. After months of talking, Sommer was in the final battles of letting go of a consuming guilt that taunted her since the sixth grade.

I looked at Sommer's common childhood struggles as innocent in comparison to my long list of what might seem like *bigger* sins. But the enemy wasn't so merciful. He heaped ongoing condemnation within her mind. *You are such a liar. You call yourself a Christian, but then you said that bad word. God will never love you!* His constant lies zinged through her mind and tormented her sensitive little soul.

Sommer is the type of person who hates doing anything bad. She tells on herself if she even thinks something remotely off-putting.

I have to be honest. I felt tempted to diminish Sommer's sin and say something like "Oh, sweetheart. You haven't done anything that any other person hasn't done at some point in their life." But, Sommer didn't need my consolation; she needed assurance of God's truths and reassurance of His love.

I extended my arms. "Come here, baby-girl." Though fourteen, Sommer didn't mind me calling her my baby-girl. She pressed in against my shoulder and welcomed my embrace. For the next hour, Sommer and I talked in depth about the Father's love and Satan's tactics to distort that love.

I shared with her that the devil often says, "You'll never be enough." But God declares, "By grace you have been saved . . . it is the gift of God, not by works, so that no one can boast."[2] The enemy suggests, "God will never forgive you." Yet God promises, "As far as the east is from the west, so far has he removed our transgressions from us."[3] Satan lies, saying, "God has abandoned you and rejected you." God's Word reminds, "See, I have engraved you on the palms of my hands."[4]

As we shared together, we discussed the importance of replacing the enemy's lies with God's truth and compared the enemy's harsh condemnations with the Holy Spirit's gentle correction. We deliberated ways to hold fast to God's Word and resist defeating emotions . . . practices I hope she utilizes throughout her entire life.

"Thank you, Mommy. Will you pray now so these lies stay away?"

"You bet I will!" We snuggled closely together until the final amen. Sommer dried her eyes, kissed me on the cheek, and then skipped happily to her room.

Whew! I wish it was always that easy. I wish I could simply cite the truth and then go on my merry little way . . . but overcoming the enemy's lies is not always simple. Sometimes we go for days thinking

God has forgotten us. Sometimes we spend years chasing after anything but God. Sometimes we gravitate toward the devil's lies and then live with the consequences of our bad decisions. And sometimes, in the process, we destroy our marital relationship.

> *"Resist with the utmost abhorrence anything that causes you to doubt God's love and his loving-kindness toward you. Allow nothing to make you question the Father's love for his child."*[5]
>
> A. W. PINK

But wait! Before I move on, maybe we need to stop to consider what we believe about the devil. I mean, do we even believe he exists? Is he fictitious or is he real? If he is real, how much focus should we allocate to him?

Some give little attention to the devil, believing him to simply be metaphorical. Others give too much attention to him and find him hiding under every bush; they excuse their actions and shift their personal responsibility to accusations that sound like comedian Flip Wilson's famous excuse, "The devil made me do it."

Personally, I don't like giving the enemy much attention, but neither can I deny his existence. In the end, human opinions really don't matter; we must look to Scripture to see how God describes our arch-enemy.

First Peter 5:8-9 warns us, "Be self-controlled and alert. Your enemy the devil prowls around like a roaring lion looking for someone to devour. Resist him, standing firm in the faith." John 8:44 describes him as the father of all lies. In Luke 4, the devil had the audacity to tempt Jesus. In John 10:10, Jesus describes him as the thief whose mission is to steal, kill, and destroy.

Today, that mission hasn't changed. Since the beginning of human existence, the devil has sought to destroy. Satan is deceptive in all his ways, a master of manipulation. He constantly bombards, consistently stalks, and incessantly attacks our minds. Through books, television, and worldly advice God's arch-enemy looks for the opportunity to take us down by telling us lies about who we are, what we need, and what we should value. He knows his best overall attack is to hit at the heart of the church—attempting to destroy the family unit through broken marriages.

Think about it. If you wanted to knock out the lights of a major city, which would be more efficient—unplugging light bulb after light bulb, or going directly to the power plant? Of course the answer is the latter. Thus, if we embrace Satan's lies within our marriages, he destroys our whole families, influencing not just our life but many other lives. He truly is the thief who comes "to steal, kill, and destroy."[6] Oh, we may not see him visually, but his whispers echo throughout our society as he craftily stirs dissension by mixing truth with deception.

What are some of his whispering deceptions? What lies echo throughout our culture? And, most importantly, have we embraced any?

Some of the enemy's most common lies in marriage are:

- You deserve to be happy.
- It doesn't hurt to look.
- You deserve better.
- If your spouse really loved you, they would . . .
- Getting a divorce is no big deal.
- A true Christian marriage just happens . . . it doesn't take much effort.

My friend Patty complains, "I'm just not happy anymore. I don't think I can go on." Her vows uttered at the altar to love, honor, and cherish are long forgotten. The enemy now entices her with whispers of *'Life is too short; you deserve to be happy. You will be better off if you just leave.'* True, life is short. True, God wants us to live joy-filled lives. The deception, however, occurs in accepting divorce as the only solution, or in accepting that happiness and fulfillment will be found in anything other than a surrendered life to Christ. Divorce doesn't bring instant peace. Instead, it often exchanges lives of turmoil while living together, with lives of turmoil while living apart.

> *"Divorce answers no questions, solves no problem, resolves no conflict, gives no respite, restores no dignity, and grants no peace."* [7]
>
> DENNIS AND BARBARA RAINEY

Sarah is miserable, but vows to stay committed to her marriage. She mulls over all the ways Jake disappoints her. "My marriage isn't fair. I give, and give, and give. Jake only takes! If he really loved me, he would take me to dinner or go for walks, like we used to." Her thoughts give way to martyrdom and self-pity. She believes she is the only one who sacrifices; she occupies her time with keeping score instead of embracing God's truth that love "keeps no record of wrongs."[8]

> *Not seeing your spouse's concessions doesn't mean they don't exist—maybe you simply fail to recognize them.*

Mike, married to Carol for twenty years, can't take his eyes off Heather as she saunters into the office. *Whew! I remember when Carol looked that hot.* Trena, married for six years, also faces sexual temptation. She tries to ignore her feelings, but every time Dante smiles, euphoria runs through her veins. She thinks to herself, *If only Seth looked at me that way.* Both Mike and Trena play a dangerous game of emotional roulette, thinking someone else will satisfy their longings. They dismiss their flirtations as "innocent" and embrace the lie that "it doesn't hurt to look." They ignore the sad reality that marriages end every day from thoughts starting out much like theirs. They forget how nobody awakes to a foreign thought of, *I think I'll have an affair today.* Instead, their thought begins with an idea that, when entertained long enough, leads to action. The action, no matter how justified in the thinker's mind, always produces a wake of turmoil, despair, and pain.

> *The devil subtly whispers, "If it feels good, do it. No one will know." But instead of asking, "Can I get away with this?" consider, "Is this a wise decision?" When there's a doubt, do without!*

Then there's my friend Cindy, who confides over coffee, "I just don't feel anything for Ricky. Honestly, I don't know if I ever loved him." Somehow, over time, something has skewed Cindy's definition of love.

In our culture, we *love* everything from deep-dish pizza and bubble gum to watching *Dancing with the Stars* and Monday night football. Children as young as grade school begin texting or writing notes containing affectionate *I love you*s. We've reduced love to preference and euphoria. But real love is an active choice, a commitment rather than mere feeling. We don't fall in and out of it in an instant; it involves great effort and intentionality.

Don't get me wrong: After fifteen years of marriage, working side-by-side in business, and spending countless hours with my husband, I still get butterflies when he holds my hand, or looks at me with that mischievous grin I've come to adore. But my love for him is far greater than a giggle in my tummy or a flush of adrenaline through my veins. I am committed to Greg . . . for better or worse . . . for richer or poorer . . . in sickness and in health. And so is he toward me.

As I reflect on the lies my friends entertain, I want to shake them from their slumber and say, "Wake up! Can't you see where this type of thinking leads? God wants so much more for you and your marriage."

A Powerful Truth

Secret #4—If you want to enjoy a marriage filled with friendship, laughter, and genuine love, you must resist the devil's lies by embracing God's truth!

Perhaps one of the greatest lies the enemy traps us into believing is that a blissful marriage just happens naturally. Everything in our society cries out for instant gratification. From microwave ovens, instant potatoes, and fast-food meals guaranteed in less than five minutes, to surgeries making us look ten years younger or pure extract pills guaranteeing our loss of ten pounds, we desire instant gratification that demands little effort. We believe the lie that our marriage won't take effort. Our modern-day fairy tale reads like this: "Once upon a time there was a really hot prince and a smokin' hot princess who had everything money could buy. They enjoyed luxury, fame, and a fat bank account. They traveled at will and were the envy of the town. Everyone wanted to be like them. They fell blissfully in love, enjoyed red-hot sex, and lived happily-ever-after . . . without any work or sacrifice."

Okay. So this story may be a little exaggerated, but probably not too far off. And the sad part is, we believe it.

Lest I project myself as having it all together, let me confess: I entered marriage with an expectation of being fulfilled, not with an attitude of fulfilling. I expected perfection. I thought Greg would know exactly what to say and when to say it. I thought he'd always be suave and debonair. I didn't realize Greg would have his own ideas and expectations. I served so many others that quite honestly I lived with the expectation that marriage would be the one place I could have my needs met. I focused on the idea that I deserved to be happy, and believed that good marriages just happen.

However, I quickly discovered this powerful truth: you get back what you put into your relationship. And really great marriages take a lot of hard work and intentionality.

"I think a lot of the time we take relationships for granted. Because of that, we don't always give them the attention they deserve or require. But good relationships require a lot of effort." [9]

JOHN MAXWELL

When Greg and I first married, I finally learned that just because two Christians marry does not mean they'll automatically enjoy a Christian marriage. A Christian marriage takes as much commitment, energy, and determination as our own spiritual journey with Christ, maybe even more. But when we embrace the challenges posed throughout our marriage and serve our spouse as Christ served the church, we reap rewards well worth the sacrifice. True joy manifests as we serve one another as unto God, when we lay down our rights and wash one another's feet. Practically put, I live and offer everything in my power to make sure Greg's dreams come true, and he gives his full concentration to ensure mine.

Now that's a marriage worth fighting for!

Better than a fairy tale or a fly-by-feel-good relationship, Scripture defines marriage as a union, a sacred covenant typified by the relationship Christ shares with the church. God describes marriage as a communion involving three: a man, a woman, and God. Marriage takes commitment. It requires our vow to serve and love unconditionally. If we commit to love God, then we follow His command to love our spouse; and if we love our spouse as God loves us, selfish ambition dies.

As I contemplated Christ's life and death, I had to question everything I once believed about love. I asked myself: Did God's Word shape my beliefs, or had I adopted the world's standards concerning love? I also considered Christ's selflessness. Christ never said, "Sorry, Father, I don't think I'm going to die on the cross today. I don't deserve this treatment. I deserve to be happy. I never asked for any of this. I don't deserve to be crucified." Instead, He emptied Himself and gave up His life to serve. He washed the feet of his betrayer. He whispered, "Father, forgive them, for they do not know what they are doing."[10] He released his entitlement and lived to please the Father. His identity rested securely in the Father's opinion, not a fickle mob's. His love remained faithful, steadfast, unmoved by circumstances.

Boy, did I ever need to make some changes—beginning with the realization that *life is not about "me."* Like Christ, I exist to glorify God, to live unto Him, and to fulfill His commands.

> *"'If any man will come after Me,' said Jesus,*
> *'the condition is that he must leave something behind,'*
> *his right to himself. Is Jesus Christ worth it, or am I one*
> *of those who accepts His salvation but thoroughly*
> *objects to giving up my right to myself to Him?"* [11]
>
> OSWALD CHAMBERS

So, how about it? Do your thoughts align with God's, or have the devil's subtleties crept in?

The enemy whispers, "You deserve to be happy." God says, "I alone bring fulfillment and I created you to glorify me."[12]

The devil says, "You deserve better." God says, "Delight in your spouse."[13]

The enemy suggests, "It doesn't hurt to look." God says "If you look upon another person lustfully, you've already committed adultery in your heart."[14]

The devil mutters, "If your spouse really loved you, they would . . ." God says, "Prefer one another's needs over your own."[15]

The enemy insinuates, "Getting a divorce is no big deal." God says, "What I have brought together, let no one tear apart."[16] Why? Because God knows the pain that accompanies a disintergrated marriage.

What do you believe? Have you bought into the enemy's lies? Do any of your thoughts contradict God's Word?

Questions to Ask

1. Do I entertain the lie of, *Life is too short, I deserve to be happy; I will be better off if I just leave?* How does this thinking clash with God's Word? Stormie Omartian writes, "If you believe enough lies, your heart will eventually be hardened against God's truth."[17] Ask yourself: What does a hard heart look like? Have I hardened my heart towards God's Word and opened my beliefs to accept the enemy's lies?

2. Do I have a *martyr* mentality, thinking, *My marriage isn't fair. I give, and give, and give. If my spouse really loved me, he would do X, Y, or Z.* Truthfully, we seldom recognize our blind spots. Human tendency focuses on the areas where we feel slighted or short-changed. Projecting a victim mentality comes easily. But to make a marriage thrive, we need to ask God, "What changes can I make to better my marriage?" "How can I make my spouse's dreams come true?" "How can I honor You and my spouse every day, in every way?"

3. Have I allowed an open door for the enemy by entertaining thoughts like, *Someone else will satisfy my soul's longing?* In his book *How to Win Friends and Influence People,* Dale Carnegie writes: "It isn't what you have or who you are or where you are or what you are doing that makes you happy or unhappy. It is what you think about it."[18] Ask yourself: "Am I playing a game of emotional roulette by entertaining inappropriate thoughts of others? Am I opening my life for compromises that could destroy my relationship? Do I meditate only on my spouse, or do I fantasize about others?"

4. Have I reduced love to euphoric feelings, entertaining thoughts like, *I just don't feel anything for my spouse anymore. Honestly, I don't*

know if I ever loved him/her. C. S. Lewis said, "Love is not affectionate feeling, but a steady wish for the loved person's ultimate good as far as it can be obtained."[19] Do I prefer my spouse's feelings over my own? *yes, for most part*

As we examine our hearts, it is important to evaluate how our concept of love compares with God's truth. His Word offers us a clear definition of love and instructs us how to experience fuller, more intimate relationships. Take a few moments to meditate on the following Scriptures and consider the following verses.

Verses to Consider

1. Proverbs 16:2 says, "All a man's ways seem innocent to him, but motives are weighed by the LORD." This passage implies that we sometimes deceive ourselves, justify wrong actions, and don't even realize it. Ask, "Do I seek after God with a sincere heart and rely on His Holy Spirit to keep me from making mistakes? Do I provide opportunities for God to speak and reveal areas I need to surrender, or am I too busy to listen?"

2. First John 4:16-21 records, "God is love. Whoever lives in love lives in God, and God in him. In this way, love is made complete among us . . . There is no fear in love. But perfect love drives out fear . . . We love because he first loved us. If anyone says, 'I love God,' yet hates his brother, he is a liar. For anyone who does not love his brother, whom he has seen, cannot love God, whom he has not seen . . . Whoever loves God must also love his brother." Now ask yourself: "Do I love like this, or do I impose conditions on my love?"

3. First Corinthians 13 describes love: "Love is patient, love is kind. It does not envy, it does not boast, it is not proud. It is not rude, it is not self-seeking, it is not easily angered, it keeps no record of wrongs. Love does not delight in evil but rejoices with the truth. It always protects, always trusts, always hopes, always perseveres. Love never fails." Meditate on 1 Corinthians 13; read it as if for the first time. Ask yourself: "Am I demonstrating love like this in my marriage? What changes do I need to make? How can I love more like Christ loves me?" *→ Anger / Annoyance*
Record of wrongs → patience

4. First Corinthians 10:6 warns us to not set our hearts on evil things. God always provides a means of escape from temptation (see 1 Cor. 10:13). One of the best ways to avoid temptation is by instilling healthy boundaries. Women possess a keen sense for picking out potentially dangerous women, and indeed husbands need to pay attention. But ladies, remember to heed your husband's warnings too. Your male friend from the office may entertain more than platonic thoughts, especially if he appears overly understanding and empathetic. Protective boundaries need to be put in place. Do you need to pull away from any potentially dangerous relationships?

5. As Christians, God commands us to love unconditionally as He loves us. In John 13:34-35 Jesus says, "A new command I give you: Love one another. As I have loved you, so you must love one another. By this all men will know that you are my disciples, if you love one another." If we want lasting marriages, then we must build them upon the fundamental principles found in God's Word. We must not allow the enemy a foothold by entertaining divorce as an option. Ask, "Am I guarding against all subtle attitudes that oppose the wedding vows I made before God?"

> *If you're not feeling love toward your spouse,*
> *there comes a point where you must decide that your*
> *commitment is more important than your feelings.*
> *But, be encouraged. Your choice to love often*
> *rekindles the feelings associated with love.*

At one point I remember asking myself, "What do I really want?" More than my desire to be loved, I wanted Greg to know he was loved. I wanted to be cared for and nurtured, but I resolved that whether I ever felt cherished or not, I would love sacrificially. I chose to demonstrate my love by remaining silent when I wanted to retaliate. (At least most of the time!)

In *How to Win Friends and Influence People,* Dale Carnegie writes, "By fighting you never get enough, but by yielding you get more than you expected."[20] I considered, *Do I really want to squabble to get my way, or should I shower Greg with kind words of respect and love?* When I chose to do the latter, I found I needed to stress my point of view less; Greg became attentive to my needs. He inquired after my opinions. He sought my advice. He became more sensitive to my desires.

Was it easy? No!

Was it worth it? Yes!

But I wasn't the only one who offered love unconditionally. Greg made huge changes too.

Greg's Turn

Throughout history, thought leaders including King Solomon, Earl Nightingale, Napoleon Hill, Maxwell Maltz, and many others have emphasized that we become what we think about. It's a simple truth that most ignore. Most never even stop to consider what tapes play in their head.

Let's face it: Society feeds us a constant stream of falsities concerning relationships and marriage. From the airbrushed models of Hollywood to the *if-it-feels-good-do-it* mentality, we can buy into the fantasy and lose sight of reality if we aren't careful. These idealistic lies can be extremely damaging. They slip in unnoticed. I wonder sometimes if they aren't the biggest threat to marriage as God designed it.

In addition to the lessons Julie noted earlier in this chapter, we also made conscious decisions to set healthy boundaries. Most were pretty practical but, to our surprise, not all that common. But hey, sometimes you have to go against the grain.

First we considered what shaped our thoughts. Was it the Bible? Was it our friends? Was it life experience? Was it television, books, or music? We concluded the answer was, yes! Whether we meant it or not, all of those factors shaped our paradigm.

You've heard the old saying, "Trash in, trash out," right? Well, Julie and I made a conscious decision to install our own filters. We stopped watching certain television shows and cut out R-rated movies. I limited the amount of country music I listened to and replaced it with Christian radio. We scheduled Bible time and implemented a weekly date night. We began to consider which friendships supported our growth and which ones held us back. It was important to cut certain things from our life—but equally important was what we replaced them with. At first it seemed like a sacrifice, but over time, it was simply an exchange of habit.

When's the last time you took inventory of your life?

A friend once shared a simple but profound statement, "What we feed grows; what we starve dies." What are you feeding? Maybe more importantly, what are you starving?

I needed to learn to starve the lies and feed the truth. I needed to replace lies such as *Ah, it's not that big of a deal. I'm a harmless flirt. It's just a little joke. I don't mean anything by it. There's no harm in looking.* I replaced these lies with the truth from God's Word about honoring your wife so that your prayers won't be hindered[21] . . . about not letting a coarse joke come from your lips[22] . . . about accepting that if a man looks upon a woman to lust after her, he has already committed adultery in his mind.[23] I guarded my actions by asking, *If my wife were here, would I tell the same joke? If my wife were looking through my eyes, would she be pleased with what I'm looking at? If my wife were here, would she feel honored?*

How about you? What messages secretly play in your mind? When compared with Scripture, do your thoughts line up with God's? Take time to consider His thoughts today, and you'll enjoy the freedom found in surrendering to Him.

A Letter from the Father

Dear Child,

Hear Me. Listen to My warning.[24] Be on guard; your enemy seeks to destroy and entice you away by your own lusts.[25] He masks himself as an angel of light, but his "wisdom" is steeped in lies filled with selfish gain.[26] His ways seem right, but in the end produce death.[27]

Commit your ways to Me and experience true satisfaction and joy.[28] Follow after the example of My Son.[29] Seek Me, that you might know the truth and live in the fullness I provide.[30] I will put a new heart in you, one that craves after Me and rejoices in the truth.[31] I will enrapture your heart and thoughts with My presence and grant you true wisdom.[32] *Delight in Me and experience My fullness.*[33]

I delight in your obedience.[34] *I rejoice over your faithfulness.*[35] *My plans are to fill you with the fullness of My life and the joy that comes in knowing Me.*[36] *In this world you will be tempted and tested.*[37] *But each time you choose to listen and obey, each time you take up your cross to follow Me, you will receive from Me what can never be taken away—the joy of My salvation—the security of My faithfulness—the joy of My love!*[38]

Closing Prayer

God, please forgive me for accepting any of the enemy's lies. I know Satan aims to destroy my marriage; so God, please help me experience marriage as You intended. Heal and comfort my wounds.

I commit myself, my spouse, and our marriage to You. We desperately need Your presence. I know You are able to change me and my spouse; make our wills to be like Yours. Remove our stubbornness, our pride, our selfishness, and help us to forgive and love each other as You forgive and love us. Each time we want to speak or think hateful thoughts, remind us of the love You hold for each of us.

Jesus, You loved us so much that You died for us. I know the sins separating us are more of an offense to You than they are to one another—yet You forgive us freely. Help me, help us to do the same. Let us love one another in action. Help us to love with all of our hearts.

You promised to give wisdom to all who ask. I ask You for wisdom. Give me discernment so I can avoid falling prey to the enemy's lies. I desire to love my spouse. Help me never to entertain divorce as a simple option for my marriage. Help me to not keep score of wrongs but to freely forgive.

Guard my heart. Never allow me to entertain improper feelings or emotions for others. Knit me together with my spouse; help us always to be faithful to one another in mind, body, and soul. Finally, help me to demonstrate unconditional love. I know love is not just an emotion, it is an action. I choose to love my spouse.

Help me walk out Your love in truth with a sincere heart. Make my marriage thrive.

I pray, in Jesus' name. Amen.

For Your Reflection

Don't be naïve; we live in a world at war! Satan seeks to devour us. His goal is to fill our minds with lies and to cause us to believe them. But God is greater than Satan. The One who is truth can vanquish all lies.

Just because two Christians marry does not mean they'll automatically have a Christian marriage. A Christian marriage takes as much commitment, energy, and determination as does your own spiritual journey with Christ. Embrace the challenges posed throughout your marriage, and serve your spouse as Christ served the church. If you'll do this, you will reap rewards worth far more than the sacrifice.

A Practical Application

Be aware—Satan is your true enemy. His tactic is to steal, kill, and destroy; he wants to destroy your marriage by deceiving you. He is the father of lies. So resist his whispers:

"Life is too short; you deserve to be happy."

"Your marriage isn't fair. You constantly give; your spouse only takes; if your spouse really loved you, they would . . . "

"Someone else will satisfy your soul's longing."

"You don't feel anything for your spouse anymore. Maybe you didn't ever love them."

Instead, meditate on your spouse's good qualities. Every time you see them do something kind, write it down on a piece of paper and thank God specifically for their sacrifice. Find a way, each day, for the next seven days, to do something special for your spouse.

Most of all, overcome and resist the enemy's lies by refuting them with God's Word. Commit to memorizing one Scripture every week for the next four weeks. Then, when the enemy murmurs his lies, you will be able to refute them more powerfully.

A Moment for Preparation

Transformation occurs when we let go of preconceived ideas of what should have been and collectively work toward one another's best interests, serving in all humility.

Andrew Murray wrote, "It is easy to think that we humble ourselves before God, but our humility toward others is the only sufficient proof that our humility before God is real."[1]

Do you assert the attitude of, "I will take care of my spouse's needs when they take care of mine?" Remember, marriage isn't about focusing on your own personal needs; it's about serving and having the maturity to meet the needs of your spouse.

REPLACE
UNREALISTIC
EXPECTATIONS

*"Trust in the LORD with all your heart and lean not
on your own understanding; in all your ways acknowledge him,
and he will make your paths straight."*

PROVERBS 3:5-6

Imagine while sitting in a hotel lobby, you overhear a couple bickering. You try to resist eavesdropping, but oddly enough, the couple doesn't seem to mind being overheard.

"Harry, why don't you love me? We've been married over fifty years. And, in all those years, you've never once walked across the room to get me a glass of punch like other men do for their wives."

You listen intently. Her voice begins to elevate, pleading for her husband's affection. "I just don't understand! I'm not asking for much. Yet you refuse to meet this simple request."

A few seconds pass; the woman speaks again: "Harry, I wish you loved me! Would you please, just this one time, get me something to drink?"

Finally, he responds. "Mabel, why do you always do this to me? Why do you insist on asking me to serve you like this?"

You try to mind your own business but can't help thinking, *Man, what a jerk. Seriously, Harry? If you really loved Mabel, why wouldn't you do something so simple?*

After several more minutes of listening to their heated exchange, you can't take it anymore and decide to get involved. Walking across the hotel lobby, you decide to get her a glass of punch. But as you come around the tall pillar that has been blocking the couple from your view, you notice something alarming—Harry is in a wheelchair; he's paralyzed from the neck down. Harry isn't self-centered or egocentric after all; he simply isn't physically capable of meeting Mabel's desires.

Perspective makes all the difference, doesn't it?

Obviously, if confronted with this scenario in real life, we'd tell Mabel, "Get over it. Don't be offended!"

Yet how often do we project unrealistic expectations into our own marriages? How often do we become frustrated when our spouse doesn't deliver what we perceive to be simple gestures of love? Could it be that their life's battles render them incapable of meeting our expectations? Could our expectations, though simple, be unrealistic?

Whether our conflicts are gigantic or minute, confrontations typically result from unmet expectations.

"Believe me, you bring who you are to your marriage. So understanding your mate's history is vital to understanding the dynamics of your marriage." [2]

SANDRA ALDRICH

One of Greg's and my silliest arguments occurred while completing a questionnaire in a couples devotional book. The question read something to the effect of *Complete this sentence: "I wish my spouse was better at . . ."* It should have warned, *Stop before you fill in the blank! Do not, under any circumstance, tell your spouse your answer until they prepare themselves to hear it.*

Of course, you already know, from reading this book so far, what I wrote down! I wanted Greg to spend more time at home with me and the kids and less time fishing. I'd shared the same request a thousand times before.

Greg knew this was coming—and even welcomed it. He admitted it was an area he was willing to work on. I told myself this was turning out to be a great night. I just *loved* our devotional time . . .

Then it was Greg's turn to answer. Honestly, I couldn't imagine he'd have anything to say. "Okay, baby, what do you wish I did better?" I asked earnestly. *I was so perfect in every way.*

Greg smiled affectionately and responded. "I wish you cleaned the house better."

I literally laughed out loud. Not just a little chuckle but one of those hearty, belly-shaking, robust laughs. I truly thought he was kidding.

But he wasn't!

An instant blood-boiling rage overtook me. I was livid! "You have got to be joking. I change all the diapers. I do all the laundry. I cook! I clean! I stay up all night with the kids while *you* sleep! Then . . . I work a full-time shift of forty hours, every week, only to start the whole process over again! And *you* have the *audacity* to wish I cleaned the house better?"

Greg had made his statement innocently and without malice, but I wasn't prepared to hear his answer. And I certainly wasn't ready to meet his request for a more domesticated wife.

A Powerful Truth

Secret #5—Understand the origin of one another's expectations, and work to cultivate realistic expectations together.

Greg had grown up so differently from me. His upbringing shaped his expectations for marriage, including his beliefs about our roles and obligation, just as mine did. He felt frustrated if dinner wasn't ready on time and disappointed if dust appeared between the spindles of our dining room chairs. I didn't care about the tidiness of our home; I just wanted to spend time together.

Greg's dad, brother, and stepdad shaped him, leaving their fingerprints on his life. The same is true of my family—my mother and sisters shaped who I became. We hold their traits, good and bad, as they hold ours.

True, at the wedding altar we leave our families of origin to become one flesh with this new person. But becoming one in mind and heart requires a process. By understanding our families' beliefs and our responses to our families' norms, we better avoid confrontations and create new expectations.

In her book *Men Read Newspapers, Not Minds*, Sandra Aldrich writes, "Kati and Ken were arguing, as usual, about who should take out the garbage. The compromise method wasn't working because each thought the other should automatically handle that responsibility. It wasn't until they were continuing the argument over coffee with an older neighbor that they saw what was really happening. 'Wait a minute, you two,' the neighbor said. 'When you were growing up, who always took care of the garbage?' Kati answered, 'My dad,' just as Ken said, 'My mom.' The neighbor grinned.

'So you're both assuming that your home will be run by the same habits? Sounds like you two need to do a little more talking.'"[3]

We typically look at our family and decide either we want to be just like them or vow we'll never do things the way they did. These expectations, spoken or unspoken, become part of us.

Bridgette's father abused her physically and verbally. She vowed to create a different home environment for her children. She makes her mindset clear these days by saying, "Children deserve the right to express their thoughts. They need to be nurtured." But Bridgette takes her vow to extreme measures. She ferociously attacks her husband, Ed, at the mildest correction of their children.

Tina can't understand why Mike won't put his dishes in the dishwasher instead of leaving them on the dining room table every night. "I've asked him a hundred million times to put them up," she declares to our small group. "My father always helped my mother with the dishes, but Mike won't even carry them to our sink!"

Tiffany wonders why Paul runs water the entire time he brushes his teeth. "It's such a waste," she exclaims as she rolls her eyes.

What expectations cause confrontations in your marriage? Take a moment to consider the following questions.

① Family Interaction/Involvement
② Money
③ Church
④ Communication ✿

Questions to Ask

1. How would you describe your spouse's household? How does your spouse describe his father and mother? Were both parents present in the home? Did they practice gender-specific chores? How did your spouse's parents communicate with one another? How did they spend money? Who made the final decisions? Did the father or mother work all the time?

Turmoil, drug addicts/absent, jail, moms

The more we understand our expectations and their origins, the more likely we will resolve conflicts between us.

2. What actions do you appreciate about your spouse? Or, what values do you wish they shared in common with you? Now, lest you break out in an argument—don't share your thoughts with your spouse quite yet, at least not until you process the *whys.*

Caregiving, Support, affection, etc... - conservation/point/logic

3. *Why* do you wish your spouse managed finances differently? *Why* do you wish they showered you with gifts? *Why* is it so important that they believe or act in a certain way? *Why* is it their responsibility to wash the dishes (or some other chore)? *Why* are you frustrated at certain actions they do or don't do? Do any of your *whys* stem from your upbringing? Could there be an equally good (merely different) way of operating your household?

After evaluating your spouse's upbringing, take a moment to consider yours. Decide whether or not your expectation is realistic by asking: Does this expectation line up with the principles taught in God's Word? If it contradicts the Word of God, then get rid of it. If the Word of God supports the expectation, then keep it.

Look at it from a practical standpoint as well. Is it possible for you to meet your spouse's expectation? If it is ethical, balanced, and feasible, then why not compromise and choose to serve?

Expectations often remain unmentioned because we aren't aware of what we've adopted as normal.

Your confrontations may be big, they may be small—ours were both. Recognizing where your conflicts originate is important. Decide together on realistic expectations. If an expectation is attainable, then change; always try to meet your spouse's need.

Many times we fail to meet the needs of our spouse because of pride. We determine, "I will take care of his needs when he takes care of mine." But if we want thriving marriages, we must stop focusing on our own needs and commit to focusing on meeting theirs.

"I think if I could help a new wife in any area, it would be to discourage her from coming into her marriage with a big list of expectations and then being upset when her husband doesn't live up to them. Of course there are some basics that should be agreed upon before the wedding date, such as fidelity, financial support, honesty, kindness, basic decency, a high moral standard, physical and emotional love and protection."[4]

STORMIE OMARTIAN

Of course, God intended certain expectations to be kept in any marriage relationship, regardless of upbringing—marital faithfulness, honesty, and commitment, for example. God's Word expounds and supports these expectations. Other expectations, however, must be judged, weighed out, and at times dismissed.

Marriage is about giving and continuing to give even when you don't feel you can give anymore. Cultivate and practice servanthood within your marriage relationship. The more you serve, the more likely your spouse will serve and reciprocate your actions. Developing positive habits creates and cultivates a deep relationship of love and commitment, but it has to start somewhere. (Since you are the one reading this book, I guess it starts with you.) Remember, servanthood isn't a matter of self-will. True servanthood originates from an intimate relationship with God. His love will empower you to serve from the heart in an ongoing, sustainable manner.

When Greg and I began to understand where the majority of our marital conflicts originated, it became a fun game to discover one another's unwritten and unspoken needs. We embraced our different worlds and together claimed our own. We decided together how to spend the money and how to discipline the children. He went fishing less, and I took more pride in cleaning the house. (Ironically, I am now a "neatness freak," and Greg often encourages me to simply sit down and spend some time connecting with him—a direct result of our devotion to understanding one another's needs and expectations.)

"Treat a man as he is, and he will remain as he is. Treat a man as he can and should be, and he will become as he can and should be." [5]

STEPHEN COVEY

God's Word provides powerful insights to experience greater intimacy. Consider the following Scriptures and your attitude towards them.

Verses to Consider

1. Colossians 3:17 says, "Whatever you do, whether in word or deed, do it all in the name of the Lord Jesus." Do you serve your spouse based on their merit or God's? Remember, ultimately, God is the One we serve.

2. Philippians 2:3-4 encourages us to "do nothing out of selfish ambition or vain conceit, but in humility consider others better than yourselves. Each of you should look not only to your own interests, but also to the interests of others." How can you demonstrate this kind of love to your spouse? *Run Both, Compliment, open doors, Pump gas, pay bills, etc.*

3. Galatians 5:13-15 warns us to "serve one another in love. The entire law is summed up in a single command: 'Love your neighbor as yourself.' If you keep on biting and devouring each other, watch out or you will be destroyed by each other." Are there any areas in which you haven't loved your spouse as yourself? Are there any ways you need to serve more like Christ? *Ignore our personal feelings & Serve first*

In their book *The Seven Conflicts*, Tim and Joy Downs write, "The truth is, almost seventy percent of our conflicts are perpetual. These disagreements return to visit us again and again in different forms because we fail to recognize the underlying issues that fuel them."[6] Greg and I began to understand that the expectations we carried into marriage weren't necessarily *right* or *wrong*; they were simply expectations needing to be understood.

Greg's Turn

Okay, so if you read this chapter, you're thinking I'm a pretty big jerk. And for that, I have no real defense . . . except . . . Julie insisted that I fill in the blank! We really do laugh about it now, and my, how the tides have turned. We may have the cleanest house in town!

There was another expectation that caused confrontation in the early years of our marriage. It started with a belief I acquired when I was a kid.

I must have been about eight or nine years old. My parents had separated and divorced. I remember hearing a lot of banter from my parents and close relatives concerning the whole ordeal. After the divorce, my mother met someone while she was in the hospital for tuberculosis. One day, I heard my grandmother (whom I worshiped) say something to the effect of "she chose that man over those kids."

While I don't remember the exact context, I do know that I misinterpreted her meaning for years. It was one of many comments that I would use to form a paradigm, which I carried into my marriage, concerning the hierarchy of children in marriage. I believed that children were supposed to be top priority under any circumstance. Since I had formed this opinion largely based on something my *godly* grandmother said, I decided it was biblical! It's not. At least not the way I held it in my mind.

Certainly our children are a priority. If it comes to who would eat or go hungry, I think most of us would agree that the kids would eat, right? However, let me give an example of where I was wrong.

Julie was tired; she had been working and taking care of the kids. We'd both been very busy. She was looking forward to spending some desperately needed quiet time together that evening.

The kids had other plans. Courtney in particular felt she should be able to stay up with us. Like most kids her age, she used every trick in the book to pull at our emotions to get her way. If you have children, you know the routine. The problem was that Julie and I had a difference of opinion. I can't recall the details of the heated argument that followed, but I remember the most important one. At one point, I looked at Julie and firmly made this statement. "Let me make something perfectly clear to you: My kids will always take priority over you. You will always be second to them!"

What a horrible thing to say! Julie was taken aback, to say the least. With tears in her eyes she responded, "That's just not right, Greg. That's just not right!"

No matter, I was convinced that I was on the high moral ground.

Looking back now, I believe there was a sense of guilt that permeated my parenting. My oldest daughter, Courtney, had endured the divorce between her mother and me. As a result, Courtney had gone through a lot of painful changes. It was the last thing in the world I wanted my children to go through. I felt guilty. Have you ever parented out of guilt? If so, I encourage you to consider if you really believe it's an effective way to prepare your children for the real word. If we are honest, it's actually selfish.

A few months later I was talking with a more seasoned friend at work. Somehow we landed on the topic of marriage, children, and parenting. I shared my opinion of the hierarchy at home, which I had already begun to question. I wasn't prepared for his response.

"Greg," he said, "one day your kids will move on, and they should. It's the way God designed it. They'll move away, marry someone, and begin a life of their own. Long after they are gone, Julie is still going to be there. You better get your priorities straight—or she may not be."

Huh? . . . I hadn't thought of it that way. I was immediately convicted, and went to Julie and apologized for my ignorance.

Over the years, I have learned to examine my belief system. It's a rewarding thing to do. If what we believe isn't challenged, how do we really know what we believe?

Today, I encourage you to consider what beliefs you may have that are untrue. Specifically, what are the events that shaped your beliefs concerning marriage? I believe when we examine and interrogate our beliefs, we learn that some of our expectations are unfounded and may be causing confrontations. Ask these questions with your spouse in an unthreatening environment, and laugh at both the similarities and differences.

Some of the beliefs Julie and I used to carry were not only hilarious but, when examined, clearly misplaced. Julie and I have found this to be some of our most fun conversations. It allows us to get in better touch with ourselves and our belief system. We learn more about each other. We grow, and as a result we revise the expectations that cause confrontations, and we leave a much healthier legacy for our children.

A Letter from the Father

My Dear Child,

Will you trust Me? Will you follow after Me? Will you love as I have loved you? Allow me to empower you with My Spirit.[7] Seek Me, that you might find life and hope for your soul.[8]

Don't demand your way; be humble and I will grant you grace.[9] Be gentle and patiently serve.[10] Make every effort to live according to My Spirit.[11] For in My Spirit, there is fullness of life.[12] Seek peace and pursue it, and My ears will be attentive to your prayers.[13]

Be careful not to follow after worldly wisdom; bring your thoughts in line with Mine.[14] Consider and follow My ways, and you will not be ashamed.[15] Remember My commands and be faithful to do them; then you will be blessed.[16] Though the world instructs you to declare your rights, I have provided you an example to follow after: Serve as I have served you.[17]

Have nothing to do with self-love, pride, or ungratefulness. Don't be unforgiving, conceited, or lovers of pleasure; rather, be a lover of Me.[18] Indeed, there will be ways seeming right to you, but in the end they produce only death.[19] My words are filled with life and will bring forth a joy unspeakable, full of my glory.[20] Follow Me, in order that you might live.[21]

Closing Prayer

Father, help me to walk in humility. Cause me to see the world not only through my own eyes, but also through Your eyes, and the eyes of my spouse. Help me humble myself and offer compassion toward my spouse. I want to understand what he/she thinks and how he/she feels.

Help us resolve our conflicts and reach a middle ground of understanding with one another. Knit us together as one. Let our pasts be simply that, our pasts. Help us create new habits and develop a family structure founded on Your Word. Grant us the ability to leave a legacy of love for our children.

May my spirit and agendas never cloud the path You desire for our marriage. Likewise, may my spouse yield to Your will for us. May we surrender all of our expectations in exchange for Your sovereign will. Make our marriage thrive.

I pray in Jesus' name. Amen.

For Your Reflection

Many marital arguments stem from expectations formed in childhood. You can avoid a lot of arguments by understanding the origin of one another's expectations and working toward cultivating realistic expectations together.

Here's a good rule to follow: If the expectation is attainable, meet the need. Remember, marriage isn't about selfishly focusing on your own personal needs; it's about serving and having the maturity to meet the needs of your spouse.

A Practical Application

One horse, I've been told, can pull 9,000 pounds. But when you yoke the horse with another horse of the same stature, they can actually pull 27,000 pounds. Instead of pulling twice as much, they exceed their individual potential by working together, which produces astounding results.

Our marriages are the same. Philippians 4:8 tells us, "Whatever is true, whatever is noble, whatever is right, whatever is pure, whatever is lovely, whatever is admirable—if anything is excellent or praiseworthy—think about such things." Take a moment to believe the best about your spouse.

Write down three expectations you desire from your spouse on paper. Discuss the roles each of your parents played in their marriages. Are there similarities in your expectations?

When confronted with an unmet expectation, choose to extend mercy. Ask God to renew your mind and bring peace to your relationship. Then decide on one way, every day, to demonstrate love to your spouse. ① Emotionally Supportive/Encouraging ② Budget/Save pay bills ③

A Moment for Preparation

Transformation begins in our heart and the private meditations of our thoughts. We will experience greater joy and fulfillment in our relationships as we train our mind and speech to stop saying harmful words and practice the daily discipline of believing and speaking encouraging words of affirmation. As Erich Fromm, the German social psychologist, once said, "Love is possible only if two persons communicate with each other from the center of their existence." [1]

Ask yourself, "Do I speak intimately with my spouse and strive to listen to their innermost thoughts and passions? Or, have I succumbed to ho-hum conversations containing little to no value? How can I intentionally communicate more deeply and add value to my spouse?"

TAME YOUR TONGUE

"If anyone considers himself religious and yet does not keep a tight rein on his tongue, he deceives himself and his religion is worthless."

JAMES 1:26

Working alongside my husband proved advantageous. Greg's ability to "read" people was extremely beneficial.

"Listen to me, Julie. Tom's known for making *every* female supervisor who's ever worked for him cry. Don't let him! He'll attack your character. He'll demean you. He'll heighten your emotions by saying just about anything to get you worked up; it's his tactic of keeping the upper hand." I listened intently like an athlete on the sideline receiving a play-by-play from the coach.

Greg spoke quickly and in a matter-of-fact tone. He didn't have much time. Tom had called our meeting and given me only five minutes to prepare.

"Stick to the facts," Greg continued. "Don't get caught up in emotions. When Tom elevates his voice . . . and he will . . . take a deep breath. If you need to, think of something else. Let your mind drift from the conversation. I know how intently you try to listen to people, but this time you're going to need to ignore when he becomes belligerent. When he lowers his voice and appears to calm down, restate the issue at hand and keep to the facts."

I clung to every word Greg spoke and determined to become the first female supervisor Tom couldn't make cry.

Honestly, if there had been a reality show to discover the worst boss in America, Tom would have won easily. I'm not sure what caused his hatred and unprovoked assaults, but he was relentless. Anyone who worked for him knew of his mood swings—completely jovial one moment, and an absolute tyrant the next.

The meeting went just as Greg predicted. I almost laughed out loud a few times, when Tom said verbatim what Greg foretold. I watched as Tom's eyes tightened and the veins on his neck popped. Everything happened exactly like Greg said it would: "You're incompetent! You're the worst supervisor I've ever worked with. You have no idea of leadership."

Each time Tom snarled, I took a deep breath. When I felt tears forming in the corners of my eyes, I shut out Tom's words and thought about something else. Each time Tom exaggerated and twisted the situation, I maintained my poise. I chose to remain unemotional and spoke only the undeniable facts pertaining to the topic at hand.

". . . I can't believe you received so many Spotlight Leader Awards. You'll never lead anyone effectively. Your skill sets are worthless!" Tom's tyrannical insults ended abruptly when the Human Resource director, along with three other team members, knocked on the window to our meeting room. Whew! Were they ever a welcome sight!

I smiled and realized I had done it. I had passed the test. I had refrained from speaking evil. I hadn't exchanged insult for insult. When

Tom provoked me, I hadn't retaliated. When he snarled irrational ultimatums, I had remained calm.

I wish I could say the same for my conduct when Greg and I first married. Ugh! That was a completely different story. Someone should have clued me in on marital confrontations the way Greg prepared me for my meeting with Tom. I wish I had prepared what I would or wouldn't say. I wish I had guarded my emotions or devised a plan not to run off on wild, emotional roller coaster rides every time a disagreement arose in my home. I wish I had known the vital secret of how to tame my tongue.

A Powerful Truth
Secret #6—Control your tongue by allowing God to tame your heart.

Don't be mistaken; your words can cut your spouse like any other person. Your speech can bring death to your relationship—or bring life.

How do you speak to your spouse? How do you speak about your spouse? What thoughts fill your mind? Know this—what you hide in your heart eventually surfaces.

Let's face it: Taming our tongue seems simple . . . until we are provoked, right? But seriously, the familiarity of marriage leads us to say things to our spouse we would never dare say to another human being.

Self-centered thinking and self-seeking notions instigate disparaging words.

A woman named Charity is mild-mannered and never says a cross word to anyone publicly. Yet during a small group meeting she asks for prayer. "I can't seem to refrain from being cynical toward Geoffrey. I loathe everything about him. I find myself saying things I later regret, but at the time, I can't seem to stop."

Martin screams at Nicole, "You're such a ----. No wonder you don't have any friends." Nicole retaliates, "Well, you'll never amount to anything! You're a complete waste of breath!" The crazy thing is, Marty's a great guy, and Nicole is a complete sweetheart of a friend. But something snaps inside them and causes them to spew words they'd never dare utter elsewhere.

They want to be kind. They don't want to attack. But each feels powerless to the swirling emotions stirring within them, raising the imminent question of *how*? How do you change conversations laced with accusation? How do you modify feelings ensnared by personal needs? How do you speak words of affirmation instead of retaliation?

If you want to control your speech, you must control your thoughts.

Matthew 12:34-35 offers this insight: "For out of the overflow of the heart the mouth speaks. The good man brings good things out of the good stored up in him, and the evil man brings evil things out of the evil stored up in him."

During my college years, I met an incredible older couple named Andy and Bella. I loved watching them interact. He consistently opened her car door. She joyfully carried his dinner plate from the dining room table. I marveled how Bella hung on every word Andy said. I wondered how many times, in their forty-eight years of marriage, she had heard him tell the same story. I personally heard it at least ten times in the short eight months of our friendship. Even so, I loved watching the two of them together. Bella giggled like a schoolgirl, and at times her face actually turned a soft pink because of the crush she still felt whenever Andy looked her way.

"Does Andy ever do anything to irritate you?" I asked. "I mean, did you guys ever fight or say cruel things to one another?"

They looked at one another and chuckled. "Oh heavens, yes!" Bella replied. "Of course! But at some point it just became a waste of energy. After all, neither one of us was going to go anywhere, so we decided we'd better learn how to get along."

Words can be like the pressure valve on a steam cooker that lets off steam. Or the arrow through the bull's-eye that heals a wounded mate. Words are powerful.[2]

PATRICK MORLEY

Watching Bella and Andy, I realized I wanted what they had, but I wondered if it was possible for my life. During the first years of Greg's and my marriage, I began to ask a lot of self-reflective questions, such as: What do I need to do to ensure we get along? How can I speak words of affirmation instead of words of affliction? How do I truly control my speech?

Questions to Ask

1. One of the greatest checkpoints I implemented to help me control my speech was when I learned to ask myself, *Will this offense matter five minutes from now?* If it did, I followed it with a second question. *Will this matter five years from now?* I committed to address the issue only if it counted past the immediate present.

Ask yourself: "Do I tend to feel compelled to speak every thought? Do I speak every emotion? Do I feel the need to discuss every problem?" If so, ask God to help you not sweat the small stuff.

> *"The same sentence can have two different meanings, depending on how you say it. The statement 'I love you,' when said with kindness and tenderness, can be a genuine expression of love. But what about the statement, 'I love you?' The question mark changes the whole meaning of those three words. Sometimes our words are saying one thing, but our tone of voice is saying another."* [3]
>
> GARY CHAPMAN

2. I also realized that taming the tongue isn't merely keeping it *from* saying something, but also training it *how* to say something. As a trainer with a telemarketing company, I knew the importance of voice inflection. Different inflections imply different meanings. For example, at the end of a phone conversation, if Greg says "Love ya," his words imply a generic tone of

a simple good-bye. If he looks at me fondly while rocking our kids to sleep and whispers, "I . . . love . . . you," his words imply a deeper commitment. And when he feels frisky and wiggles his eyebrows and says, "Baby—I love you!" he implies something altogether different. So, although all of his words are virtually the same, they imply entirely different meanings. Does your tone, inflection, or volume level distract or communicate insinuations or insincerity?

3. In our relationship, I realized Greg's deep desire for respect, and though I kept saying, "I love you" with my words, I needed to learn how to say I respect you with my actions. I learned the value of changing my vocabulary to "I am so proud to be your wife." "You are an incredible leader." Or, "If anybody can do it" (the big dream he just shared), "you can!" Sentences such as these catapulted Greg's esteem. Likewise, Greg learned the value of guarding his tones and volume levels when we communicated.

What does your spouse need? How could you positively enhance your communication? Are you willing to set aside your needs and put your spouse's needs above your own by intentionally learning to offer love in the way they receive it?

4. People rise to the words you speak over them. If you tell your spouse they're a no-good scoundrel who lacks empathy—you'll probably get just that. But if you choose to shower your spouse with words of affirmation, they'll rise to the occasion. Praising and believing the best about our spouse heals our relationship powerfully.

Ask: "Do I build and encourage my spouse? Or do my words communicate judgment and tear them down?"

5. The most important aspect of controlling our speech is controlling our heart and thoughts. Ask: "What do I constantly focus on? Do my thoughts edify, lift up, and believe the best? Or do they tear down and believe the worst about my spouse?"

"A few sincere words skillfully clumped together can lift the spirit of your partner high into the heavens."[4]

PATRICK MORLEY

Never underestimate the power of praise. I learned its value from a college professor. You see, until my freshman year in college, no one ever told me I was bright. During a summer course, my professor (who mastered in praising people) expressed his belief in my abilities. Not wanting him to find out I usually got Cs in high school, I studied diligently. His praise inspired me to do better.

Oh, my gosh! I got an A+. Me! An A+!

Dr. Best smiled. "I knew you could do it!" he said. As the result of his belief and ongoing encouragement, I finished college with a 4.0 GPA, *summa cum laude,* and number one in my class.

Isn't it amazing what a person's words can do?

Oh, of course if someone acts unscrupulously, you need to recognize it and not be blind to blatant character flaws. After all, if it walks like a duck and quacks like a duck it most often is a duck. Yet in marriage, erring on the side of mercy always triumphs over judgment. Most people simply need to receive the same type of encouragement my college professor offered to me. They need someone to believe the very best in them.

What if we practiced praise instead of sarcasm? What if we told our spouse all the ways we valued them? What if we didn't just keep our tongues from saying bad things, but actually tamed them to express words of admiration, love, and respect? What do you think our marriages might look like?

Verses to Consider

1. James 1:19 says, "Everyone should be quick to listen, slow to speak and slow to become angry." So, set aside your preconceived ideas and expectations. Listen with a willing and open heart. Ask God to give you wisdom and the ability to hear and understand your spouse. Don't speak quickly. Ask for God's words of comfort and compassion. Remember, just because we have emotions and opinions doesn't mean we need to speak every one of them.

Wives, exercise the same restraint in responding to your husband as you would if your girlfriend asked, "Do I look chubby in these pants?" Husbands, remember that just as you would never yell at a female co-worker or point out her flaws, you should act as patiently with your wife. The truth is we can control our speech—if we really want to!

2. Proverbs 4:23-24 says, "Guard your heart, for it is the wellspring of life. Put away perversity from your mouth; keep corrupt talk far from your lips." Greg's and my relationship came a long way from where it started. Initially, our words destroyed and hurt one another. But by surrendering our hearts, God seasoned our speech with love. I am thankful we learned the value of seasoning our marriage with words of love and devotion. I want to encourage you. If we can do it, so can you.

3. Finally, in Matthew 22:37-40, Jesus provides instruction for us, saying: "'Love the Lord your God with all your heart and with all your soul and with all your mind.' This is the first and greatest commandment. And the second is like it: 'Love your neighbor as yourself.' All the Law and the Prophets hang on these two commandments."

When we truly love God and allow Him to meet our needs, He refines our thinking and changes our character to be like His. We love more perfectly, and our speech reflects it.

Greg's Turn

I used to have a horrible temper. I owned it, too. I proudly excused it away like some family inheritance. "It's my Irish/Indian heritage coming out." "You don't want to mess with a Gorman." "I've never backed down from a fight." I bragged about my ability to cut people down to size. What an immature idiot!

It would take years to come to my senses and change my reckless conduct. I remember so many times when Julie and I fought, and the more I spouted back insults or tried to make my point, the angrier I got. The angrier I got, the more explosive the result. I was working myself into a fury. Thankfully over time, I learned that this was not a quality anyone preferred in a friend, let alone a mate.

I remember when God began to deal with my heart on this issue. We had just left church. I overheard Julie mention that she needed to go by the mall to exchange a pair of shoes. "Let me drive you there so you can get it taken care of, babe," I volunteered.

Like I said, we just got out of church so I was on my best behavior. Julie hesitated. Taking three small children into the mall was never a good experience, at least not for us. Leaving them alone in the car with me was certain to be worse. I mean, these were three little kids. Courtney was around six, Sommer would have been two, and Joshua was a newborn.

"I'll drop you off, and you can run in by yourself," I insisted. "I'll stay in the car with the kids." After a few words of encouragement, she reluctantly accepted my offer.

Well, the mall was apparently busy . . .

The longer we waited, the more restless the children became. Sommer squirmed around like a worm on a hot sidewalk. Joshua spit up. Courtney was hungry. You know, all the normal little-kid stuff. I became impatient. I remember thinking, *Oh I am going to let her have it when she comes out.* I actually rehearsed ways I could describe my horrific experience to maximize the effect of my sacrifice. The truth is—it really wasn't horrific at all. Our kids were just doing what kids their age do. But there I sat, plotting my attack.

As the story in my mind got juicier, suddenly it hit me, *What's your motive here, Greg? What outcome are you hoping for? Is this really how you want to treat your wife? You're the one who talked her into going in!* No wonder she had been reluctant. Here I was planning to do my very best to ruin her day.

Who does that? What kind of person would treat another human being this way? This, however, was not just another human being; this was my wife. My pattern of thinking needed to change.

Julie walked briskly out of the mall toward the car. As she opened the door, I could tell she was bracing herself for my reprimand. "I'm so sorry," she said. "It was busy in there. They couldn't find my size. I tried to hurry as much as I could."

My response surprised her. "No problem, babe. The kids were actually pretty good." And so began the first steps of taming my tongue.

I am amazed at how far we have come. For years I had looked for offenses, kept score, and logged each affront into my consciousness, preparing for a shootout. When the time was right, with my

GREG AND JULIE GORMAN

ammunition fully loaded, I had blazed a relentless rapid fire until I knew I had left her defenseless. Unfortunately, I hear of all-too-many couples who do the same. What sense does that make?

The Bible tells us in Proverbs 18:21, "Death and life are in the power of the tongue, and those who love it will eat its fruit." Which fruit do you want to enjoy? I'm thinking I want life, a big ol' plate full of life!

You may be delighted to know that today Julie and I very rarely exchange harsh words. In fact, I cannot remember the last time we did. I encourage you to look at your spouse. Do you see them? This is a human being! Have compassion. They're doing the best they can. How do you want this day to be remembered? What if today was the last you had with them?

If that's not enough to motivate you, always remember, we reap what we sow; each one of us will reap a harvest of the seeds we plant. Change your habit of thinking. Plant some good seed today.

A Letter from the Father

Dear Child,

Listen to Me.[5] *Quiet all the noise and distractions.*[6] *Silence all the busy-ness of your life and spend time with Me.*[7] *I will fill you with the truth of who you are.*[8] *I will remind you of what is most important.*[9]

True, you will be tested and face trials,[10] *but I will send My Spirit to you to assist you.*[11] *As you draw near to Me, you will experience true love, joy, and peace. You will gain greater patience.*[12] *I will equip you with kindness.*[13] *Let Me have your heart, and I will govern your speech.*[14] *Let your heart be filled with love for Me, and you will discover treasures far greater than gold.*[15]

Ask for forgiveness for every careless word, and be slow to become angry. Come and learn from Me.[16] *I will turn your rashness to gentleness and exchange your weakness for My power.*[17] *The things that once controlled you, you will overcome.*[18] *I will teach you how to demonstrate self-control in your* relationships.[19] *Offenses will fall to the wayside as you remember who I am and who I have called you to be.[20] I will teach you to love what is good and to resist what is evil.[21]*

I commit My love to you and will never forsake My faithfulness to you.[22] I am the True Bridegroom and have chosen you to be Mine.[23] Entrust your life and your marriage to Me.[24] Trust Me.[25] I will not disappoint you; you will taste of My goodness and bear the fullness of My Spirit and life.[26]

Closing Prayer

Father, I know You desire my speech to be uplifting. You desire me to think on my spouse's good qualities, not their bad ones. But I often find myself trying to push my way, plead my case, and insist that they listen to my needs. Please forgive me.

Help me think on what is good, so that the overflow of my heart speaks words of comfort and love. Cause me to focus on my spouse's good qualities and not belabor negative thoughts. I give You my speech. Guard my mouth. Help me not to use words that tear my spouse down. Make my marriage thrive.

I pray in Jesus' name. Amen.

For Your Reflection

The familiarity of marriage causes us to say things to our spouse we would never dare say to another human being. But don't be mistaken: your words cut and damage your spouse like any other person. Your speech will bring life or death to your relationship. Therefore, control your tongue by allowing God to tame your heart.

A Practical Application

First Peter 3:8-9 says, "Finally, all of you, live in harmony with one another; be sympathetic, love as brothers, be compassionate and humble. Do not repay evil with evil or insult with insult, but with blessing, because to this you were called so that you may inherit a blessing."

① Spirituality ③ Self
② Intro to love   place

1. Take a few moments to write out three reasons you love and respect your spouse. Then, find a way to daily express your admiration.

2. Express your respect and love in the way they will most effectively hear you. (Practice doing this for thirty days, and you will create better habits.)

3. Set up new rules in communicating. Before you confront your spouse, ask these questions: "Will this enhance our relationship or tear it down? Does this really need to be addressed? Does it impact anyone eternally? How would Christ handle this situation?"

4. If a conversation with your spouse turns volatile, refrain from giving your opinion. Instead say, "Since you deserve the best, I want to make sure I support you. So, let's table this conversation and pray about it for a while." Then ask God to help you love your spouse and to communicate love and respect. Submit your thoughts, emotions, and speech to God. He will help you control your speech. Seek Him first. Allow Him to fill you with His presence and refine your character to be more like His.

5. Learn when to remain silent. Wives, we tend to express our emotions frequently and in detail. Be cautious to pick optimal timing. It's not effective to share your desperate need for compatibility after your spouse says

his boss yelled at him today and ten of his employees threatened mutiny.

Husbands, when your wife is busy helping the kids with homework or faces urgent deadlines, it probably isn't the best time to ask, "Why isn't the house clean?" or "When will dinner be ready?" Look for ways to help, without resentment. If your spouse is tired, don't ask them to stay up all night watching movies. If they feel like a failure, it may not be the best time to say, "Well if you did X, Y, or Z, you wouldn't be in this situation." We're not saying you should neglect necessary conversations; simply delay the subject matter until an optimal time. If need be, schedule a set time to talk in the near future, so you both know resolution is coming. Make sure you both possess the energy to focus on the conversation. Schedule an early dinner date in order to spend time alone.

A Moment for Preparation

Transformation begins when we focus on what is essential and then intentionally practice the good things we know to do. As Christians, God requires us to love—our love is a spiritual act of worship. True love is mature, committed, and selfless.

The Christian marriage is incredibly unique, because God charges both husband and wife to demonstrate their love for one another—like He demonstrated His love for us. Deborah Smith Pegues wrote, "Emotional intimacy is the bedrock of any meaningful and rewarding relationship. Without it, relationships become shallow and unfulfilling."[1]

Ask, "In what ways can I intentionally connect with my spouse and set aside time to connect and communicate my love and respect for them?"

BE INTENTIONAL

"If two lie down together, they will keep warm. But how can one keep warm alone? Though one may be overpowered, two can defend themselves. A cord of three strands is not quickly broken."

ECCLESIASTES 4:11-12

I remember the first time Greg officially asked me out. Walking by my work station, he said, "Whatcha doing tonight?"

"Going home to watch a movie," I replied.

"Oh yeah, with who?" Greg probed.

Chuckling, I responded, "No one."

I'll never forget his confident reply: "No, you're not—you're going out with me!"

With butterflies fluttering in my stomach, I couldn't help smiling. "Well, okay," I giggled.

Everyone loves euphoric moments, when emotions and chemistry ignite feelings of absolute joy and excitement. If you're like me, you want to fan those feelings to flames. When we first meet

GREG AND JULIE GORMAN

our dream boy or dream girl, we foster euphoric feelings by searching for their good. We look for every opportunity to find similar qualities for connection. We dress to impress. We put our best foot forward. We search to understand and celebrate the other person so as to capture their affection.

But over time, if we aren't careful, we settle into mundane activities and forget to practice the wonderful gift of discovery. Day-to-day tasks steal our attention. Then, we begin to notice all the little ways our partner irritates us. We begin to wonder, *When are they going to take care of my needs?* And, if we aren't intentional, over time we forget the most important part of the relationship—one another.

Granted, there are only so many hours in the day. But whether we are surviving the life-stage of sleepless nights and small children, or navigating the middle years of career and family, or reflecting on where we've come from as we sort through emotions of an empty nest, we must intentionally guard our relationship and not take our spouse for granted.

A Powerful Truth
Secret #7—*Live intentionally to stay connected.*

Shellie and Tony spent the early part of their marriage ministering together. When the kids came along, Shellie threw herself into nurturing their growth and became less available for community outreaches. Tony continued to focus more and more on outward opportunities.

But as his love for others grew, his connection with Shellie diminished. Tony worked longer and longer hours, while Shellie poured herself into their kids. A gap began to grow between them.

In Shellie's mind, there always seemed to be another expected sacrifice. Her needs always took second to the needs of others. She felt guilty if she said anything … after all, her desires seemed so small in comparison. The demands of "the urgent" interrupted date night after date night. Tony's indifference planted seeds of loneliness in Shellie. Over time, resentment grew. Bitterness matured.

A similar offense took root in Tony's thinking. Ballet recitals, football games, and homework seemed to consume all of Shellie's energy. By the time he arrived home in the evening, he needed Shellie to connect with him, but she lived perpetually exhausted. Their love-making became virtually nonexistent. Their formerly vibrant affection for one another turned to superficial conversation. They became content to watch the world pass by out of two separate windows.

Tony and Shellie aren't alone. Adrian and Nikki once functioned on just a couple hours of sleep because they couldn't get enough of one another. They'd talk until the wee hours of the morning. Now they barely connect, except an occasional brush of shoulders, walking opposite directions, in their hallway.

> *"Marriage isn't about the final destination—*
> *the happily-ever-after with the person of our dreams.*
> *It's about the journey—getting there, walking together,*
> *enjoying the adventure en route to our final destination:*
> *a true sense of oneness with the other."* [2]
>
> CINDI MCMENAMIN

Jamie and Stephanie blame one another. "You cheated first!" Jamie shouts. Stephanie exclaims, "Yeah, right! What about all the years you couldn't get enough of porn channels and men's magazines? They don't count, right?"

Then there's Mitch and Melanie. Neither one of them have the energy or the desire to place blame. They simply want out.

Sadly, each story started out with a hope for the happily-ever-after. But does *happily-ever-after* ever just happen? In *Rekindling the Romance: Loving the Love of Your Life*, Dennis and Barbara Rainey write: "New love is easy. Happily-ever-after life is hard work."[3]

So, how do some marriages seem to thrive, despite insurmountable obstacles, while others seem doomed from the wedding night? Answers can be discovered by reflecting on the following questions.

Questions to Ask

1. Dr. John C. Maxwell, an extremely successful world leader, has written this fundamental principle: "To add value to others, you need to start putting others ahead of yourself in your mind and heart. If you can do it there, you will be able to put them first in your actions."[4] If we want healthy, vibrant relationships, we must intentionally put our spouse's needs above our own.

Ask yourself: "Do I value my spouse's feelings, thoughts and dreams? Do I seek to serve them and communicate admiration? Do the majority of my thoughts focus on what I need, or what my spouse needs? When my spouse thinks of me at the end of the day, would they say I made them feel valued?"

2. My dear friend Tammy Maltby shares, "Being BUSY means *Being Under Satan's Yoke*." How do we know when we are busy? It's when the pressing of the urgent takes precedence over

what matters most. Our relationships struggle when we fail to position them with the importance they deserve.

So guard your time to connect. What distractions do you need to remove in order to add value to your relationship? Social media? Entertainment? Your career? Have you preoccupied your time with less important matters rather than focusing on what matters most? Are there ways you could slow your schedule to make time to connect with your spouse? The truth is, time hasn't changed. We still have twenty-four hours in our day. The question remains: Will we use our time intentionally for our spouse, or squander it on less important matters?

3. Communicating intentionally means planning time for it. Greg and I plan a date night every week. And because of the intensity of life's demands, we spend time each morning talking, planning, and strategizing over a cup of coffee. We've discovered that dating, plus this time of connection, interrupts our mundane routines and keeps our lives moving in the same direction.

So are you ready to get really honest with yourself? If so, ask, "When is the last time I surprised my spouse by arranging a date night and planning to do something I know they'd enjoy? Do I practice looking and acting my best like when we first dated? Do I foster flirtation to win my spouse's affection and attention?"

God designed us for relationship. His Word offers powerful insights for married couples.

Verses to Consider

1. In Ephesians 5:21, Paul encourages married couples to "submit to one another out of reverence for Christ." As I looked into the possible meanings of *reverence* here, I ran into the Greek word *phobos*, which literally means fear or "reverential fear of God," "a wholesome dread of displeasing Him," "a fear that influences the disposition and attitude of one whose circumstances are guided by trust in God, through the indwelling Spirit of God."[5] In simple terms, we submit to one another because of our love, devotion, and "reverential fear" of God. Our submission is mutual because we are all subject to Christ.

We submit as our spiritual act of worship to God. It is not something we do when we *feel* like it; we submit regardless of how we feel. Submitting to Christ is the key; godly submission never requires you to do something contrary to God's Word. Never define submission as mindless obedience.

2. In Ephesians 5:22-24, Paul addresses wives by saying, "Wives, submit to your husbands as to the Lord. For the husband is the head of the wife as Christ is the head of the church, his body, of which he is the Savior. Now as the church submits to Christ, so also wives should submit to their husbands in everything." The Scripture says to respect our husbands. Again, this word is *phobeo* in Greek. God's Word instructs us to submit respect to our husbands because of the position Christ gave them; our husbands hold the position as the head of our marriages (under Christ's rule.)

In her book *For Women Only,* Shaunti Feldhahn writes, "Just as our men can choose to demonstrate love toward us even if they don't feel it at the moment, we can and should choose to demonstrate respect toward them."[6]

3. Finally, in Ephesians 5:25-28, Paul instructs men: "Husbands, love your wives, just as Christ loved the church and gave himself up for her to make her holy, cleansing her by the washing with water through the word, and to present her to himself as a radiant church, without stain or wrinkle or any other blemish, but holy and blameless. In this same way, husbands ought to love their wives as their own bodies. He who loves his wife loves himself.""

Husbands, I honestly think your task is the tougher one. To love as Christ loved is an incredible commission—one that I will defer to Greg to tackle.

Greg's Turn

To "love as Christ loved the church" is an endless discussion. So I'll keep it simple. I am charged to love Julie, and my words and actions should bear witness to it. I think it really is that simple. Do I love my wife? My words and actions should be evidence enough.

This requires intentionality, which one dictionary defines as "the trait of thoughtfulness in action or decision."[7] This definition is appropriate for our discussion here. So often we are guilty of spending more thought and time preparing for a meeting with our boss than we ever do for our spouse, which makes no sense when we stop to think about it.

It alarms me when I see couples I've admired who are divorcing in a season of life when they should be enjoying the very things they worked their whole lives together to accomplish. I often wonder, *How does that happen?*

Truly, I think it happens because we get comfortable. We start out trying to impress and win the heart of our mate, but after a while, our attention drifts. Particularly as men, once we catch our prize, we can lose interest. Like a child who outgrows a toy, our attention turns to careers, kids, and television.

In my work as a certified coach, I facilitate Life Plans with some of my clients. One of the projects we tackle is determining what we need to manage *for* and what we need to manage *against*. In other words, what are the activities we have to make sure we plan to do consistently to achieve the desired result? From here, we schedule and formulate a realistic plan to be sure the client does these things.

With respect to marriage, Julie and I schedule date nights in advance. We have done this for years. It's part of our schedule. Sometimes we have to be flexible, and there are times we miss it, but rarely. The important thing is that we spend time together frequently and that we plan to do so. We are deliberate and intentional about it.

Many times we do things that cost little to no money. We go for a walk. We watch waves crashing against rocks at the beach. We grab an ice cream and sit talking, just something simple to get time alone together. Other times we may do something more elaborate.

I've learned she likes when I ask her questions and practice listening. I listen to her tell me about her day or week. I try hard not to interrupt or offer *fix-it* solutions. I focus on discovering her again and again. I have come to love this time as much as she does.

Guys, please don't make your girl plan this! Take the reins and schedule it yourself. Call her up and literally ask her out on a date as if you had just met. This is a practice that will keep you in touch with one another over the long haul. (And I am also pretty sure you're going to be pleased with the immediate results as well!)

Next, let's consider what we have to manage *against*—things that pose a threat to the desired result. What are the biggest threats to your marriage? Once you've taken the time and been honest with yourself, plan how to manage against these threats.

Your situation may be different, but for me, it's usually career-related. Sometimes I have been guilty of thinking I'm *doing it all* for Julie and the kids. That's really not true. What's closer to the truth for me and most of you is that we work and achieve just as much for our own satisfaction and ego as for our family's well-being. That's okay; I believe it is how God designed us. The other just sounds like a great comeback when my family complains that they haven't had enough quality time with me.

When I catch myself in this mindset, I have to manage against it. How? Feed the truth and starve the lie. Learn what threatens your happy, healthy marriage, and be intentional about managing against it. If you were to look at my planner, you would see certain days when I remind myself to do something thoughtful for Julie. It's my way of planning to be intentional and deliberate. When we are together, I practice being present rather than being distracted by thoughts of things I need to get done.

In addition, I have found she hears me differently when I think of new ways to say I love you. As an example, try saying it like this: "You're the one I love." You'll want to put some thought to what makes your girl tick. But with a little intentionality and "thoughtfulness in action," I think you'll find the effect well-worth the time invested.

A Letter from the Father

Dear Child,

Slow down. Breathe. Rest in Me.[8] Every day, many things grab for your attention. Quit striving and remember what is most important.[9]

The fool runs after his own wisdom.[10] The arrogant make plans in their heart and never give thought to Me.[11] But you were destined for so much more.[12] I never designed you for misery.[13] I want to clothe you with My strength and cover you with My peace.[14]

Choose what is better.[15] Love as I have loved you.[16] Serve with all humility, for I esteem the humble of heart.[17] Who do you desire to impress? Who will you serve—yourself or Me? By choosing what is better, you will taste what is best and will know the joy found only in Me.[18]

I will lead you.[19] When you feel like demanding your way, ask Me and I will give you a new heart.[20] When you feel hurt, betrayed, or disappointed, surrender it all to Me in prayer, and I will strongly support you![21] Whoever loses his life for My name's sake will find it.[22]

With all My love,

Your heavenly Father

Closing Prayer

Father, make our love new. Give us the ability to serve one another in love. Help us enjoy one another again. Let us grow together instead of apart. Renew our commitment. Help us to be sensitive to one another's needs. Let spontaneity flow in our relationship. Assist us to support one another unselfishly.

Don't allow anything to hinder me from communicating with my spouse. Aid me in the ability to be light-hearted. Alleviate any tension building between us. Let Your peace reign in my marriage, and cultivate a mature, life-giving atmosphere in this home. Cause my marriage to thrive.

In Jesus' name. Amen!

For Your Reflection

Guard your relationship. Don't take your spouse for granted. Live—intentionally—to stay connected. Take time to grow together. Seek the opportunity to add value to your spouse. Remember, the Scripture that says "A man reaps what he sows"[23] applies to every aspect of life. Consider what you've been planting. Taking time to connect renews your love for your spouse and helps you rediscover the reasons you married. Connecting intentionally restores friendship and allows time to communicate on a deeper level.

A Practical Application

Do you feel disconnected? Do you feel alone? Are you tired of the same routine? When is the last time you shared a meaningful conversation with your spouse? Do you know what your spouse dreams about? Take time to reconnect daily. Try these helpful hints to get started:

1. Think of an activity your spouse would feel is the perfect date. If possible, plan it for them.
2. Flirt with your spouse. Send them a little note telling them how much you admire them, listing specific qualities you appreciate. Nibble on their ear. Give a wink or pat. Laugh at their joke. Be genuinely mesmerized by their insights.
3. Stimulate positive interaction with thought-provoking and fun questions about things they love or have interest in, and listen with sincere interest. Find out their favorites: food, beverage, snack, candy, smell, and hobby. Talk about their favorite memories. Stimulate conversation on topics they are interested in.

A Moment for Preparation

Transformation fails when we seek our own way, fail to take responsibility for our own actions, and selfishly insist on gratifying our own desires. But when we look to meet our spouse's needs, and look for opportunities to nurture growth through our affection and affirmation, we invite connection as God intended between a husband and wife.

Dagmar O'Connor wrote, "Ninety percent of sexual problems aren't sexual at all—they have their roots in the emotional barriers we place between ourselves and our partners." [1]

Ask, "Have I allowed anything to rob me from enjoying the intimacy God intended for my marital relationship? And am I willing to let God change me so that I can express myself more freely with my spouse?"

PURSUE INTIMACY, NOT JUST SEX

"The man and his wife were both naked, and they felt no shame."

GENESIS 2:25

Darlene leaned in, raised her eyebrows slightly, and lowered her voice to a whisper. "So, you're a writer? Whatcha writin' about?"

Ahhhhhh. I don't feel like talking with anyone. I thought. *Please just leave me alone!* I was tired, frustrated, and ready to be home, but my canceled flight had left me stuck in the Cleveland airport. It was cold, rainy, and the airport shuttle bus smelled like socks worn for a week but not washed. The last thing I felt like doing was engaging in polite pleasantries.

But it seemed I had no choice. Darlene refused to divert her attention.

"I'm writing a book on marriage and the things I wish my mother had told me," I answered half-heartedly, hoping Darlene wouldn't be intrigued.

"Really! Wanna know what my mother told me on my wedding night?" Darlene answered with half a grin. Her face flushed with the excitement of a kid preparing to ride their first rollercoaster. I didn't have the heart to say no.

"Okay. You baited me. What?"

Darlene's hazel eyes widened as she grinned from ear to ear and recounted her story. "On my wedding day, my mother burst into my changing room, just before I walked down the aisle. She slammed the door behind her, and stated very frankly—'Tonight, there are some things you need to know about sex. First you're gonna have to do it. Second, you won't like it. And third, it's gonna hurt'—and then whisked out the door."

"What? You're kidding me!" Everyone on the smelly shuttle bus laughed hysterically. "Maybe I should title the book, *What I Wish My Mother Hadn't Told Me about Marriage*."

Though I doubt many of us heard advice like Darlene's mother offered her (at least I hope not), I do believe most of us encountered other distorted guidance on the subject of sex. From one generation to another, faulty messages have skewed God's intent for sexual intimacy in marriage. Earlier generations conveyed messages, whether spoken or unspoken, such as *Sex is a duty. Sex is dirty. Sex is something we never talk about.* Today's generation suggests the opposite extreme: *Sex is a free-for-all. No one saves themselves for marriage. Enjoy sex with anyone you find mildly attractive. Do whatever feels good to you!*

We live in a sex-saturated culture. Hollywood glamorizes sex and distorts God's design. When we combine society's distortion with our own discomfort over discussing it, it's no wonder dysfunction perpetuates.

We ponder, sexual . . . intimacy? The two words almost seem incompatible.

So, how about you; what did your mother tell you? Did you discuss it at all? What messages, spoken or unspoken, permeated your home, and how have those messages affected your marital relationship?

> *"There are two kinds of romantic love: emotional and physical. Both husbands and wives need both kinds of love."* [2]
>
> PATRICK MORLEY

Being raised in a family where every abuse was present, my view on sex was extremely warped. I carried deep emotional scars. Unfortunately, my experiences with men grossly distorted God's design for sexual intimacy within marriage. Practically every man I encountered validated an improper view of what a pure relationship should look like.

My skewed perceptions weighed heavily on Greg's and my relationship. I enjoyed the physical pleasure of sex, but wavered in my ability to connect with Greg emotionally. I offered an either-or choice: Connect with me emotionally or enjoy the pleasures of sex. The two never connected.

Crazy, huh? Totally *not* what God intended for oneness between a husband and wife.

Today, it's easy to write about my childhood traumas and to share how every abuse was present in my home; it has been quite another process to let go of all the damage from those years. Compound that history with the many distortions caused through my own choices, from my first boyfriend to first husband, and you might begin to capture a better picture of the uphill climb Greg and I faced. Each childhood rejection enforced my brokenness and fueled thoughts that made sexual intimacy virtually impossible. After all, intimacy isn't feasible when every private thought centers on one's self. Private harassing thoughts hampered my ability to connect. *Why am I not enough? What's wrong with me? Why can't I ever measure up?*

Although Greg affirmed his love for me, some of his past mistakes reinforced my insecurities. I forgave those mistakes but subconsciously fortified my already existing walls in an effort to protect myself. Unwritten laws governed my attitude and ability to connect. I feared abandoning myself to the sexual oneness God intended for a husband and wife.

In my previous book, *What I Wish My Mother Had Told Me About Men*, I shared a pivotal exchange between Greg and me that liberated me from these prison bars. He and I had been married a few years, and I prided myself on never having said no to his advances. *After all, that's what a good Christian wife does.*

But Greg wanted more than my *obliging;* he wanted my heart, passion, and affection. One afternoon, we entered into an intense conversation. Greg kept insisting, "Julie, I just *want* you to *want* me." By his third declaration of "I just want you to want me," I shouted, "You want me to want you? Greg, I have never said no to you!"

I thought, *Ah ha! You can't refute that one. Chalk one up for my side!*

Greg wasn't deterred. Instead, he calmly replied. "You're right. You may have never said no, Julie . . . but you've also never said yes."

Ouch! The truth of his statement smacked me in the face. His sincerity rattled the very core of my thoughts.

I had no rebuttal.

No excuse.

I was speechless.

I began to realize all the joys the enemy had stolen from me. I was so sick of my *issues!* For a moment, I grieved the innocence I'd been deprived of since adolescence. I desperately wanted God's best but felt powerless and even ignorant of what I had missed out on. I had settled for sex, not sexual intimacy. Though I never cognitively said it, I had communicated, *Greg, you can have pieces of me. You can hold my heart everywhere except in the bedroom.* During that afternoon exchange, God began to change my paradigm of sexual intimacy.

A Powerful Truth

Secret #8—God wants you to say "Yes!" to your spouse, to love them, body, mind and soul.

What do you believe about sex? Do you embrace God's design of sexual intimacy in marriage, or society's norms? Do you love your spouse with body, mind, and soul?

> *"God formed us to know no greater ecstasy than when a man and a woman literally merge into one flesh. Hormones, nerves, sensory receptors, and other specific physical characteristics are all part of His divine design for our pleasure in the physical oneness of marriage."*[3]
>
> KAY ARTHUR

Jeremy's unmistakable gaze communicates his insatiable desire for other women; yet he can't understand why Ginny won't connect with him in the bedroom. Meredith badgers Wyatt. She chastises his parenting skills. She scrutinizes his ideas; yet she questions why he refuses to be more tender and affectionate. Then there's Brian and Alissa, who approach sex with a *What's-in-it-for-me?* attitude and fail to communicate respect or love to each other.

Over the years, as Greg and I have talked with and coached couples, we've realized that sexual intimacy is desired by all but experienced by few.

So, what should the sexual relationship look like within marriage? Why do some marriages grasp and engage in its beauty, while so many others struggle to experience sexual intimacy or connect as God intended?

Questions to Ask

1. Ask yourself: "Do I use sex as a means of punishment or as a means of getting my way? Do I harbor unforgiveness toward myself, my spouse, or others concerning sex? Have I given my affection to others? Do I treat sex as a chore or obligation?"

In *Devotions for Couples,* Patrick Morley offers insights surrounding 1 Corinthians 7:5: "The Bible is clear that men and women are not to withhold sexual relations from each other unless two conditions are met. First, it must be by mutual consent . . . Second, any mutual abstinence from sexual union is to be only for an agreed-upon time, and only then so you can devote yourselves to prayer."[4]

Never stop flirting—with your spouse, that is! Great marriages readily extend grace and lavish one another with kindness, gentleness, and tender affection.

Need to work on improving ↗

2. Ask: "Do I communicate desire for my spouse, or have I reduced sex to an obligation or duty? Have I allowed anything to rob me from enjoying the intimacy God intended for my marital relationship? Do I make my spouse feel desired? Do they know they have my undivided attention and affection, both in and out of the bedroom?" *Not Sure, could do better*

In her book *For Women Only*, Shaunti Feldhahn writes, "97 percent of men said 'getting enough sex' wasn't, by itself, enough—they wanted to feel wanted."[5] Husbands, I imagine if that same survey were taken among women, the percentage would be just as high. God intended for us to connect with our spouse physically and emotionally.

3. Ask: "When I make love to my spouse, do I give them my full attention? Do I engage my body, mind, and emotions, or do I allow other faces or fascinations to distract me from connecting as God intended?" *???*

C. S. Lewis wrote, "To love at all is to be vulnerable."[6] For most of us, vulnerability is difficult. But in order to enjoy true sexual intimacy in marriage, we must be vulnerable.

Trusting and remaining vulnerable becomes especially difficult if pornography or unfaithfulness has violated the marital relationship. Upholding purity or maintaining intimacy with our spouse is impossible if someone or something else entices our attention. We can't fantasize after our spouse if another person steals our affection.

Over the years, as we've coached couples, Greg and I have witnessed the volatility of pornography's effects. It attacks the esteem of one spouse, who thinks, *If I were more beautiful, my spouse wouldn't be tempted. What's wrong with me? Why am I not enough?* Meanwhile, the other spouse remains trapped by pornography's snare and feels ashamed, disgraced, and humiliated by their lack of control.

No doubt Satan has unleashed a full-throttle attack against God's design of sexual intimacy. His tactics: airbrushed photographs and contrived videos. I was disheartened a few years ago to read these statistics: "At $13.3 billion, the 2006 revenues of the sex and porn industry in the U.S. are bigger than the NFL, NBA and Major League Baseball combined. Worldwide sex industry sales for 2006 are reported to be $97 billion. To put this in perspective, Microsoft, who sells the operating system used on most of the computers in the world (in addition to other software), reported sales of $44.8 billion in 2006."[7] I'm sure the proportions haven't changed much since then.

Indeed, the devil seeks to destroy God's design for intimacy between a husband and wife, and between the believer and God. "In a survey of over 500 Christian men at a men's retreat, over 90% admitted that they were feeling disconnected from God because lust, porn, or fantasy had gained a foothold in their lives."[8] Porn also destroys intimacy in marriage; it severs trust; it perverts God's design.

We need to resist the enemy's seductions and subtleties. We can't stop with makeshift blame, saying, "The devil made me do it. He caused all this distortion." In *Knowing God, Knowing Myself,* Cecil Murphey explains, "We don't want to face the pain of our failures. If we select another villain, we don't have to look deeply within ourselves, confess or make any changes."[9]

If pornography has taken root in your relationship, get help. Be responsible. Seek accountability. Fight for the intimacy God intended for your marriage.

In the back of this book, I list several ministries committed to helping you break free from pornography's clutch. You won't get rid of an addiction by denying it exists or pretending it will just go away. Neither is self-will enough; you need God's intervention.

Like any sin, we overcome our appetite for its temptation when we replace it with a love for God. Freedom resides in a living and loving relationship with God. As we surrender our affection to Him, we crave fleshly tendencies less. The more we exchange our thoughts for God's thoughts, the less we struggle to maintain a pure mind.

God's Word points to essential truths concerning sexual intimacy to keep the marriage bed pure—body, mind, and soul!

Verses to Consider

1. First Corinthians 7:3-5 states, "The husband should fulfill his marital duty to his wife, and likewise the wife to her husband. The wife's body does not belong to her alone but also to her husband. In the same way, the husband's body does not belong to him alone but also to his wife. Do not deprive each other except by mutual consent and for a time . . ."

Whew! Did you get that? God's Word goes so far as to say that the wife's body belongs to the husband, and the husband's body belongs to the wife. In marriage, our bodies are no longer our own. We become one with our spouse. God's Word offers clear instruction: *Do not deprive one another.* Scripture offers only one concession for not engaging in this intimate act—prayer. But the decision to "not engage" must be *mutual* and *for a set period of time for devotion to prayer.* (Fasting)

Ask yourself: "Have I used sex as a means of getting my way, by depriving my spouse as a means of punishment? Have I engaged all of my thoughts, emotions, and attention in my love-making to my spouse? Do I intentionally initiate and stay present—body, mind, and soul with my spouse in the bedroom?"

2. I love Song of Solomon 1:4, where the bride speaks to her beloved king and husband saying, "Take me away with you—let us hurry! Let the king bring me into his chambers." I also love the highly graphic passage found in Proverbs 5:15-19. Solomon encourages young men to "drink water from your own cistern, running water from your own well. Should your springs overflow in the streets, your streams of water in the public squares? Let them be yours alone, never to be shared with strangers. May your fountain be blessed, and may you rejoice in the wife of your youth. A loving doe, a graceful deer—may her breasts satisfy you always, may you ever be captivated by her love." These Bible verses are downright R-rated and reveal that God desires us to woo our spouse as King Solomon did his bride. God's Word instructs us to uphold sexual intimacy within marriage—it is among the most precious acts any two human beings share together. Ask yourself: "Am I committed to being *present* in my love-making with my spouse? Do I celebrate their physique? Do I connect with them emotionally, completely? Do I try to satisfy their needs and make them feel wanted and loved?"

"In our sex-saturated culture, the very act of living is a minefield of unwanted possible triggers and potential images that could be recalled days or years later." [10]

SHAUNTI FELDHAHN

---

3. Hebrews 13:4 insists, "Marriage should be honored by all, and the marriage bed kept pure." Ask yourself: "When making love,

do I guard and reserve my thoughts for my spouse only? Do I allow my mind to drift to my to-do list? Do I focus on their face, or do distant and distorted thoughts fill my mind? Am I thrilled to be present with them? Do I give them my unadulterated respect and my utmost untainted integrity?"

"The sexual union is a moment to drown yourself in the pleasure of one another, to be caught in the whirlpool of ecstasy that takes you deeper and deeper into one another until all is spent and you lie quietly in one another's arms feeling your oneness as never before."[11]

KAY ARTHUR

4. Ephesians 5:31-32 says, "'For this reason a man will leave his father and mother and be united to his wife, and the two will become one flesh.' This is a profound mystery—but I am talking about Christ and the church." Ask yourself: *In my marital relationship have I become one flesh with my spouse? Do I seek my way, or seek for completely inseparable connection? Am I embracing and enhancing intimacy toward my spouse? Am I cherishing their embrace, lingering in their kiss? Do I enjoy remaining by their side, relishing their touch?*

On a scale of 1 to 10, how would you rank your sexual intimacy with your spouse? Take a moment to consider how you can connect intentionally, sexually, as God intended the two of you to do.

Greg's Turn

Sex!

When you hear or say or read that word, what thought does it provoke? What emotion?

I'm not trying to be edgy here. I'm offering an opportunity for you to take an honest inventory.

So, again, clear your mind. Get quiet within yourself. Imagine a white canvas, with nothing painted on it, entirely blank.

Sex!

What was your very first thought? What emotion did it provoke? Did you feel dirty? Anxious? Hesitant? Guilty? Passionate? Peaceful? What image did you see? Was it one of love? Was it perverse? Did you envision your spouse? (If you're not in a place at this moment to answer this, I encourage you to put the book aside until you can—this is a *YOU and YOU ONLY exercise* intended to raise your awareness.)

Were you surprised at your own thoughts? If your thoughts were pleasant and biblically healthy, take a minute to sincerely thank God. If they weren't, take a moment to pray and give those thoughts and emotions to our heavenly Father. Every day hereafter, take a minute to pray for healing, and ask God for a healthy perspective concerning sex within your marriage.

Truthfully, most of us never stop to consider our emotions around sex. We don't even stop to consider where or when we picked up our view or thoughts on the matter. Sex is a topic rarely talked about in a healthy or productive manner, which is a huge problem, one that plays into Satan's hand.

But open, honest dialogue about sex is vital to our marital relationship. Communication on the subject is as important as the need for physical communion. It's a huge step toward a healthy marriage and affects many areas of life.

I recently read Napoleon Hill's classic *Think and Grow Rich*. Although the title lends itself to the topic of wealth, Hill's principles are useful for many other areas of life. I was quite surprised to find a significant portion of his book dealing with the *emotion* of *sex*.

What in the world does sex have to do with getting rich or becoming successful? Well, according to the author's study of over 25,000 people, quite a bit!

Hill, along with many behavioral scientists, builds a case that the emotion of sex is the strongest of human emotions. This is important to understand, because this force is not unlike a dammed river; the energy must be expressed. If kept dammed, it will find a release.

Now ladies, before you check out, please read on.

Men, before you jump to conclusions and grin at your wife with that *aha, I gotcha* look, please read on.

Hill notes that a man's genius is discovered when he learns to harness the emotion of sex and convert it to creative energy. His study led him to discover that most men never become extraordinarily successful until after the age of forty, or even fifty. Why? Because in their younger years most men tend to dissipate their energies through overindulgence of *physical* expression of sexual emotion. Believe it or not, men, sexual energy has uses other than, well, physical sex.

That is an interesting thought for us Type-A achievers, isn't it? I don't know about you, but I always knew there was something genius about my manhood. LOL!

Seriously though, consider Hill's thought. He writes, "Intemperance in sex habits is just as detrimental as the intemperance in habits of drinking and eating . . . Every intelligent person knows that stimulation in excess, through alcohol, or narcotics is a form of intemperance which destroys the vital organs of the body. Not every person knows, however, that overindulgence in sex expression may become a habit as destructive and as detrimental to creative effort as narcotics or liquor. A sex-mad man is not essentially different than a dope-mad man. Both have lost control of their faculties of reason and will-power."[12]

How are you doing, men? Still with me? Think about it and ask: "Am I harnessing this energy for good, or am I wasting it?"

I once heard Zig Ziglar cite a study that said men who are 100 percent committed to their wives are significantly more successful than those who leak energy and emotion into porn or sexual relations outside of marriage.

Now let it be known, it is *not* my intent to minimize our need, both male and female, for sexual intimacy in marriage. I'm simply attempting to shine a light on an uncommon thought concerning the proper use of some of this God-given energy. My prayer is for you to gain wisdom and harness some of your raw sexual energy so you can unleash your genius.

Thus, let's progress to some of Hill's other notable findings. He writes, "Marriages not blessed with the eternal affinity of love, properly balanced and proportioned with sex, cannot be happy ones—and seldom endure. Love alone will not bring happiness in marriage, nor will sex alone."[13] He goes on to say, "Fortunate is the husband whose wife understands the true relationship between the emotions of love, sex and romance."[14] The same could be said of a wife whose husband possesses the same understanding. In fact, I would say it is essential.

My own experience and studies have shown me that the strongest inherent desire of a man is to please a woman. When we learn to harness that desire, the energy enables us to discover our genius and will drive us to our highest potential.

Men, part of harnessing that energy means we focus it exclusively toward our wife. Porn is *not* acceptable. Undressing other women with our eyes *will* have a negative affect not only on our marriage but even on our work performance. The results will be truly catastrophic.

To both men and women who are parents, I'd like to propose this question: Is your paradigm of sex one that you want to transfer to your children? Whether intentional or not, it likely will be. What sort of legacy do you want to leave them concerning sexual relations? How would you coach or advise your children to have healthy view of sex? Now . . . will you turn that wisdom inward for a moment and hear your own advice?

As I write this, I am intensely aware of the different wounds many bear concerning sex. There have been hurts ranging from infidelity and porn addiction to sexual abuse. Julie had been sexually abused. We had both been promiscuous. As a result we admittedly held skewed views and emotions concerning sex. In the early years of our marriage, I confirmed many of hers.

It took a long time for me to realize that satisfying Julie meant so much more than snatching her up and mauling her. That mentality actually hurt our intimacy for several years. We had quantity, but the *connecting* quality was missing most nights. I really did want to connect with her. I just didn't understand the effect that tenderness in all my actions throughout the day would have on our time after dark. I wasn't being an idiot intentionally; I just had to learn how to be a good husband.

I was never happier than when Julie began to realize that I longed to connect with her in a special way in the bedroom. Julie was never happier than when I realized that the connection started long before we got to the bedroom! Yes, I have made my share of bedroom blunders over the years. I was an absolute jerk and an insensitive idiot at times. Thankfully Julie and I value communication, and God cares about our intimacy. This is a gift He has given us, one He truly wants us to enjoy. He offers healing when we open ourselves to receiving it.

Julie and I have learned a lot about connecting emotionally and physically over the years. I only have eyes for her. She demonstrates her desire for me, and we both honor each other with our body, mind, and spirit. We defend and protect this intimate area of our marriage. It takes work and honest dialogue, but we sure love the payoff!

A Letter from the Father

Dear Child,

I rejoice over you.[15] Draw near to Me and seek Me for help.[16] Call on Me and I will answer, in every area of your life.[17]

I designed you to enjoy sexual intimacy and oneness in marriage, without shame.[18] Listen to My instruction and celebrate sexual intimacy with your spouse.[19] Enjoy their touch. Be satisfied with their body.[20] Honor them.[21]

Do not pervert what I have created and called good.[22] Never share your love or affection with another.[23] Keep your marriage free from all unholiness.[24] Delight in your spouse.[25] Be satisfied with them and enjoy the splendor of their body.[26] Remove anything that is causing you to disconnect. Love one another with patience and kindness.[27] Protect what I have brought together.[28] Love one another completely.[29] Forgive unconditionally.[30] Prefer one another's needs over your own.[31] Rejoice in your union. Take pleasure with one another. Do not deprive one another; instead indulge in one another's love.[32] I created you for intimacy; behold, it is good![33]

With all My love,
Your heavenly Father

Closing Prayer

Father, You created sex exclusively for marriage. Fill my heart with passion for my spouse, and cause them to desire me only, as well. Grant us true fellowship in this area of our marriage. Help us engage with one another sexually. I surrender this area to You.

Help me to be playful and to connect with my spouse completely. Assist us in communicating freely about our desires and needs. Don't let our marriage bed be defiled by the filth of this world. Let it be pure. If either of us holds distorted views concerning sexual intimacy, convict us. Challenge our thinking and restore what the enemy has stolen.

I submit my mind, my body, and my heart to You. Let me live free from the perversions of this world and love my spouse as You intended me to. Keep _____ [say your spouse's name] free from temptations. Don't let my spouse be enticed or lured toward this world's distortion of sex. Cause him/her to find me exciting and appealing.

Rid me of my fears of inadequacy—and any fears about my weight, my looks, or anything else. You are God of my life; I invite You to be God of our marriage bed. Make our marriage thrive.

In Jesus' name. Amen!

For Your Reflection

As we journey to discover true sexual intimacy within marriage, remember that sex is an outward expression of the inner relationship you share with your spouse. Our sexual intimacy reveals the overall health in our relationships. If the other areas of our marriage are healthy, then our sex life will be too, and if the other areas of our relationship are not healthy then our sexual expression won't be either.

A Practical Application

Practice these five steps to foster intimacy with your spouse:

1. Intentionally connect with your spouse in and outside of the bedroom. Foster friendship and flirtation with your spouse all day. Play! Have fun! Initiate! And talk about it! Take your time; slow down. Touch your spouse affectionately, not just in the main receptive areas. Find out how you can please your spouse. Ask them what makes them feel good. Pleasure is okay—you're married.

2. Put away any form of entertainment that is distracting or destroying sexual intimacy in your marriage. Guard against anything that promotes infidelity or distorts marital intimacy the way God designed.

3. Take time to date. Thriving marriages require couples to share time together outside normal job responsibilities and family tasks. Find common interests and spend quality time talking. Do things you both enjoy.

4. Pretend it's your wedding night! How did you respond to your spouse? It may seem silly at first, but pretending it's your first night together helps you pay closer attention to the needs of your spouse.

5. Keep the lights on. Wives, our husbands are stimulated visually. Don't deprive them from looking at the only woman's body God intended and limited them to look at. If you feel uncomfortable with how you look, maybe dim the lights, but—don't deprive your husband from watching you.

Remember—God designed sex to be one of the greatest intimacies shared between a husband and wife. Love your spouse freely. Enjoy one another fully.

A Moment for Preparation

Transformation requires change. We either move toward growth to reflect more of God, or we become stagnant. The moment we stop growing is the moment we start dying. Martin Luther King Jr. said, "If you can't fly, run. If you can't run, walk. If you can't walk, crawl. But, by all means, keep moving."[1] Ask yourself, "Am I committed to move forward with my spouse, even if it means we crawl toward transformation?"

FIGHT *For,* NOT *With,* ONE ANOTHER

*"Many a man claims to have unfailing love,
but a faithful man who can find?"*

PROVERBS 20:6

"Mommy! Where are you?" Joshua shrilled.

I ran quickly to the kitchen. Something about my ten-year-old child's inflection demanded my urgent attention. "What's the matter, son?

"You need to talk with Mark's parents!"

"Why, sweetheart?"

"Well, because I chased him down and threatened to beat him up." Joshua conveyed no inkling of remorse.

I paused for a moment and then asked, "What happened? That's not like you."

Huffing and puffing, Joshua clenched his jaw and said, "Well, Mark and Ray were picking on me and Tony. So I did what you told me to do; I left. Tony followed, but Ray and Mark wouldn't leave us alone. They started chasing us, yelling and throwing sticks. I ignored them.

"I tried to brush it off, but then they made me mad; they started saying bad things about you! That's when I'd had enough! I turned my bike around, sped up to them, and rammed my tire against theirs." Joshua's eyes darted back and forth as he spoke.

"I jumped off my bike, clenched my fist, and warned them, 'You better never, ever, say anything bad about my mom again, or else!'"

I'm not sure if it's right or wrong, but I was proud of Joshua. Of course, I didn't need his defense against a couple of ten-year-old bullies, but I was proud of his character. Push Joshua to get your way, and he'll probably let you. Say bad things about him; he'll laugh it off and walk away. But say anything bad about his family, and you'll witness his absolute resolve to protect and defend. (No doubt he gets that from his daddy!)

A Powerful Truth
Secret #9—Fight for, not with, your spouse.

Isn't that how we should be in marriage? If we truly *prefer one another's needs over our own* (as Paul encourages us to do in Philippians 2), we'll take the position of servant, let our spouse get their way, laugh off silly arguments, and walk away from conversations without taking offense.

But if someone else attacks our spouse, if adversity shouts accusations to insult them . . . shouldn't we, like Joshua, defend and protect their honor?

One thing I know for certain: adversity will come. Think about the promise given to the Israelites. God promised them a land flowing with milk and honey. But, the promised inheritance wasn't given to them all at once. In Deuteronomy 7:22, God shared that He would give them the land little by little. As I reflect on their story, I realize a powerful truth: even after they crossed the Jordan, the Israelites faced battles. The promise was theirs, but they had to seize it. As a matter of fact, it was after they entered their promised land that they faced their battles. They blew trumpets and shouted around the walls of Jericho. They fought and defeated giants. Nothing happened automatically. God always invited their participation. In order to obtain their promise, they had to seize it.

Joshua and Caleb could have complained how they hadn't received their promise earlier because of the other spies' lack of belief. They could have belabored how they hadn't gotten their just dues. But instead, they fortified Israel to fight together. Israel advanced forward through a unified effort. Together, they obtained their promise. Their history teaches us that God's promise still requires our attention and unified participation.

Hardships and difficulties knock at every couple's door and bring along their entourage of fear and anxiety. When we face sickness, financial hardships, or infidelity in marriage, our response to these taunting tactics determines the outcome of our relationship.

Within the last five years, Greg and I moved across the nation—three times! We literally lived in three separate states within one year. With each move, we carefully calculated and deliberated with one another and in prayer. We made each decision with the confidence we were walking in the center of God's perfect will.

Yet for three years, we went without a paycheck. For three years, we watched our savings dwindle. For three years, we used our 401(k) to pay off credit cards and high insurance costs. We watched as our best-laid plans crashed around us. Our dreams of a *happily-ever-after* shifted to nightmares of *now what*?

Some days I wanted to curl in a corner and cower before my Goliaths. Many days I wanted to pull the covers over my head and just go back to sleep. Even more days, I felt like slipping beneath the bubbles in my tub and calling from its sanctuary, "I'm not coming out until you make this all go away!"

> *"See that you humble yourselves, and take no place before God or man but that of a servant. That is your work; let that be your one purpose and prayer."* [2]
>
> ANDREW MURRAY

During this season, where our toes dangled over the edge, and fear shouted, *Give up! It's futile! You're never gonna make it!* Greg and I faced a choice. We could lock heads and fight *with* one another, expending pointless energy on who was at fault, or we could link arms to fight *for* one another. The enemy offered plenty of opportunities for both Greg and me to shift the blame and fight with one another.

We determined we wouldn't give in, and we would never give up. I needed Greg. Greg needed me. Our kids needed us both.

Like the Israelites, we faithfully did the next right thing, followed God's lead, and defeated our giants one battle at a time. Today, Greg and I couldn't be more in love. Together, we stared down intimidation and triumphed over impossibilities. We fought adversity and reclaimed God's promised future.

We've watched other brave couples do the same. Angela determined to fast and pray for Stan's deep-seated addiction to pornography, something he had picked up from his father and grandfather. She allotted one day each week to intercede for him. She determined to release the offense to God, not taking Stan's addiction personally. Stan began to seek accountability and implemented blocks on their computer. Meanwhile, Angela offered encouragement. "God will help you gain freedom. I'm here for you! I know that if you determine to, you will overcome this!"

Cancer savaged Tina's body so terribly that her husband, Dylan, felt powerless and worn out. Cleaning up Cheerios and helping with science projects had never been his strong suit. He missed connecting with Tina. He missed her smile. Chemotherapy replaced their love-making. But Dylan remained committed. He demonstrated his love for Tina as he carried her tiny frame back and forth, from the bedroom to bathroom, when she grew too weak to walk. In time, Tina's strength returned, and she and Dylan made up for lost time.

Ellis had no idea when he said "I do" that Tiffany's family relationships would require so much sacrifice. Retirement was supposed to be the golden years, a time of free travel, a time to enjoy solitude and tranquility. But, one by one, Tiffany's children needed a place to stay; then, Tiffany's mother needed care. As car seats and walkers filled spare closets, Ellis welcomed each guest with open arms. He and Tiffany relish their time every evening as four generations celebrate meals at their dining room table.

Each of these stories found a happily-ever-after because each couple understood the powerful principle of *fighting for, not with*, their spouse.

Marriage demands a constant effort to give and give—not take and take. No matter what your marriage looks like, it can get better.

Determine not to give up; God is near. If you have breath, it is not too late to experience your happily-ever-after.

So, how about it? Do you fight *for* your spouse, or are you fighting *with* them? Do you zero in on their needs and their dreams, or blame them for everything not going well? *Little of both ↄ*

Questions to Ask

1. Tim and Joy Downs have written, "Each of us is born with an instinctive 'me first' attitude. But in marriage, each husband and wife has to cultivate a 'we first' mentality—and each needs to know that his or her partner shares that value."[3] Ask yourself: "What act of love can I practice today to build a stronger marriage? How can I encourage my spouse? How can I go to battle for them?" *①Pray ② hold hands ③hug ④ talk*

2. An interviewer once asked Thomas Edison about the failures surrounding his light bulb invention. "Edison replied, 'I didn't fail 1,000 times. The light bulb was an invention with 1,000 steps.'"[4] Whew! Can you imagine if we offered our spouse that kind of commitment? I wonder what our marriages would look like if we declared, *Failure isn't an option! I'm not going anywhere. I know it's going to take work, but we need to figure out what we need to change to get the job done.* Ask yourself: "Do I provide that kind of commitment? Do I express encouragement and dedication? Does my spouse know I am for them, not against them? Do I express ways they don't measure up, or do I defend their character and express absolute belief in their highest qualities?" *Try to. Misinterpretation/miscommunication ⓒ*

3. Oswald Chambers wrote, "Satan's aim is to make a man believe *time* that God is cruel and that things are all wrong; but when a man

strides deepest in agony and turns deliberately to the God manifested in Jesus Christ, he will find Him to be the answer to all his problems."[5] Marriage takes a lot of hard work, and at times it may feel as though it hangs by a delicate string. But God is able to mend and restore. Put your hope and confidence in Him. He won't let you down.

Jesus holds the answer for every difficulty you face within your marriage. Instead of fighting against one another and wasting your energy on who's to blame, why not ask, "How does my spouse need me to defend them today? How can I encourage them to press on? How can I, alongside them, fight for their needs, and intercede for God's desires for their life?"

Verses to Consider

1. Genesis 2:18 records, "The LORD God said, 'It is not good for the man to be alone. I will make a helper suitable for him.'" Ask: "In what ways can I aid and accompany my spouse? What one way can I demonstrate that I am with them? Am I a suitable helper? Do I nurture positive growth? Do I express kindness and support?"
   Affirmation / Positive

2. In 1 Corinthians 9:24-27, the apostle Paul writes, "Do you not know that in a race all the runners run, but only one gets the prize? Run in such a way as to get the prize. Everyone who competes in the games goes into strict training. They do it to get a crown that will not last; but we do it to get a crown that will last forever. Therefore I do not run like a man running aimlessly; I do not fight like a man beating the air. No, I beat my body and make it my slave so that after I have preached to others, I myself will not be disqualified for the prize."

Ask yourself: "Have I become lazy? Do I run aimlessly, or am I intent to win this race, arm in arm with my spouse? Do I give our marriage and relationship all I have, or have I settled for merely going through the motions? Am I just pretending to run and putting up a good front, or am I pressing on to take control of my emotional responses and practicing fundamental steps to enhance my love for my spouse?"

3. In Philippians 3:12-14, Paul writes, "Not that I have already obtained all this, or have already been made perfect, but I press on to take hold of that for which Christ Jesus took hold of me. Brothers, I do not consider myself yet to have taken hold of it. But one thing I do: Forgetting what is behind and straining toward what is ahead, I press on toward the goal to win the prize for which God has called me heavenward in Christ Jesus." In order to win, we must throw off every sin attempting to sever our relationship. Ask: "Am I fighting for my spouse, or am I still holding on to my pride, anger, or unforgiveness? How can I forget what lies behind and strain toward what God calls me to?"

Greg and I faced tough times, but we stood strong and grew together. Today, I can say with full confidence that being married to such a loving and godly man is my life's greatest privilege. Greg would do anything and give anything for me—even his life if necessary. He is a great father and an amazing companion. We laugh. We love. We dream together, and when times get tough we join our hands and rage against the battles of life together, as one. I'm so grateful we didn't give up.

We fought the good fight. We will finish the course. We have kept our faith. Our marriage, by God's grace, will stand the test of time.

Greg's Turn

Sacrifice Daily / Die Daily

Would you give your life for your wife? Sure you would, right?

Let me phrase it differently: *Are you giving* your life for your wife? Said this way, it has a different meaning, doesn't it? What do you think that means?

I'll go first.

Julie mentions a few years when we struggled with finances. This was not something we were used to. I am a very driven person who has generally earned more money each year. But not during this season.

We had been very established. I was earning a great living. We had an awesome home and were plugged in at the church. Julie had stepped away from a corporate job to answer God's call to ministry and caring for the family. Things were really going great.

Then, with much prayer and consideration, I left a very good-paying career to pursue my calling of encouraging and equipping leaders to become all they were created to be. I felt I was supposed to, and Julie agreed. We sold our dream home, packed up, and moved. We were ready for the adventure—or so we thought.

As it turned out, about the time we unpacked, we moved again. We felt a bit like Abraham; we went out, not knowing where we were going. Each stopping point held a lesson to learn or a connection that needed to be made. As we reflect, it's easy to recognize all the whys; but at the time, the only real knowing was that voice within us saying, *This is the way; walk in it.*[6] Yet, as much as we had a knowing, we also wondered what God was up to. Here we were, living in our third state in less than one year. I hadn't realized how expensive it is to move three kids, a wife, and a dog! The next two years weren't much better, but at least we were stationary.

During this time, there were multiple challenges. No friends. No church to call home. No relatives to help watch the kids if we needed to travel for business. Little to no income. I was struggling to find my purpose again. Both of us grew exhausted from the mental battle and financial pressure.

I've heard it said that heroes aren't decorated in peacetime. I agree. For our family, the chips were down. I was not easy to live with. I was depressed, discouraged, and disengaged. I lost my sense of purpose. I forgot the value of who I was and whose I was.

But Julie fought for me. She constantly reminded me of who I was. One night when I hit bottom, crying out, "I'm so sorry I've put you and the kids through all of this," she replied, "Baby, your story's not finished yet!" She constantly fasted, prayed for, and encouraged me. She believed in me when I didn't believe in myself.

Are you fighting for your spouse? When they're down, are you picking them up or kicking them? If they fail, or fall again, are you giving your spouse what they need? Are you reminding them of *who* they are and *whose* they are?

This, to me, is a large part of what marriage is about. It's not about getting our own needs met. It's about serving the other person. It's about helping them see their dreams come true. You may be thinking to yourself, "Well, Greg, that's easy for you to say; your story is all about how Julie met *your* needs." True, and that's where I prefer to keep the focus—on her. However, I will share this: During this time, Julie was working on pursuing her calling as a writer and speaker. At the time, this was not an income-generating activity. In fact, many times it cost us money. Julie sacrificed herself faithfully for those she ministered to for nearly seven years and rarely got paid. Occasionally, she received a small honorarium or love offering, but nothing that matched her worth or efforts.

On many days she offered to set ministry aside and get a paying job. At times, she felt compelled to abandon her call. I wouldn't let her. I was tempted, but I felt I needed to encourage her to stay the course and to pursue her dreams. Though I struggled with our financial constraints, I encouraged her to stay the course. Her dream of writing and speaking was coming true. I refused to let her put it aside, even though at the time, it would have been the more convenient solution.

I'll wrap up where I started. Are you giving your life for your spouse? If not, you can make the decision to start now.

A Letter from the Father

My Dear Child,

Focus your attention on Me, the Giver of Life.[7] I will sustain you.[8] I will uphold you by My righteous right hand.[9] I will offer life to you and breathe hope into your marriage and family.[10]

I am your starting point, your point of reference.[11] When you feel discouraged, I am near.[12] When you feel abandoned, remember you are not alone.[13] When you feel you can't take another step, I will carry you.[14] When you don't know which way to turn, I will instruct you.[15]

I am with you.[16] What seems impossible to you and too big to overcome is not too difficult for Me.[17] I know what you need; nothing hides from My sight.[18]

You have no idea how much I love you.[19] Your mind cannot fathom how much I have prepared for you.[20] Today, rest in My presence.[21] I have ordained your steps and will make your paths straight.[22]

You wonder what you should do; you worry about so many things. But, I tell you to rest in Me.[23] You will hear and know My voice.[24] Even when you are faithless, I remain faithful.[25] I will send My Spirit to guide you and fill you.[26] He will counsel you and show you how to live.[27] Commit your way to Me, and I will grant you the joy and peace of My presence.[28] I will do this for My name's sake and because I love you.[29]

Closing Prayer

Lord, indeed, Your Spirit is active and alive! I invite You to move on my marriage. Save it! Restore any intimacy the enemy stole from us. Strengthen me when I feel weak. Defend us in our time of trials. Teach us how to die daily to our own selfish desires and surrender our marriage to You.

Forgive me and assist me to forgive. Help me to walk humbly and to demonstrate love to my spouse. Cause me to remember and to believe the best about them.

You alone are God. You alone judge righteously without fault; remind me never to judge another person. Move on our behalf. Convict my heart of any sins causing divisions between us. May we never shift the blame to one another, but in humility cause us to serve one another. Give us wisdom to resist the devil's lies.

Help me to forget any disparaging words I've thought about speaking to my spouse. Soften my heart and tame my tongue. Establish checkpoints to keep us from quarreling, and foster a Christ-centered home. May we always live unto You and not our problems.

May our dating be filled with new life and laughter. May our marriage bed always be pure. Inspire me to never give up or give in. I desire to love my marriage partner as You have loved me. As You move on our marriage, may our love grow. Give us our happily-ever-after. Make our marriage thrive.

I pray in Jesus' name. Amen.

For Your Reflection

Marriage is a continual journey; if you struggle, you are not strange. Occasionally, every couple faces hurdles and obstacles within their relationship. Resolving to press on—together—produces healthy, satisfying relationships.

Remember, God positioned us in the heavenly realm with Christ. His wisdom is ours. His presence is ours, and our marriage is His. So, fight *for*, not *with*, your spouse!

A Practical Application

Marriage demands our constant effort of giving, not taking. Plan strategically for twists and turns in the road. Prepare for occasional accidents and detours. Position yourself for God's help by praying. Study the road map of God's Word, and you'll discover direction for your journey. You can't stop. Keep driving.

In the hazardous seasons, slow down. Remember, every journey has a starting point; your marriage started with a vow before God. Occasionally, you may find yourself at the starting line all over again, remaking and reconfirming the vows to love, honor, and serve. Recommit, always, and intentionally discover ways to put your spouse's needs before your own. Then, watch God move!

A Moment for Preparation

*Transformation occurs when we reach forward, commit to dream,
and welcome from a distance the hope of our faith. We embrace
God's promise when we let go of pessimism and self-limiting thoughts
in an exchange for God-filled expectancy.*

*God invites us to believe the best and inspire the best in our spouse.
He encourages us to invite Him into our dreams, our imaginations,
and our relationships. As Christians, we understand that faith isn't
conjuring up a noble notion and asking God to bless it; instead,
faith simply hears God's voice and then aligns to follow after it.*

*Ask yourself: "Have I stopped dreaming? What does God want
me to believe Him for again? Have I stifled my spouse from doing
and becoming all that God desires?"*

DARE TO DREAM, TOGETHER

*"If two of you on earth agree about anything you ask for,
it will be done for you by my Father in heaven."*

MATTHEW 18:19

At one time people believed the four-minute mile was impossible. Then on May 6, 1954, Roger Bannister proved them wrong. He ran a mile in 3 minutes 59.4 seconds at the Iffley Road Track in Oxford, England.[1] What was once considered impossible became the standard for all professional middle-distance runners. In the last 50 years, the four-minute barrier has been lowered by almost seventeen seconds. Apparently, once people realized they could, they did!

How about you? Are you an optimist? Pessimist? Or are you a self-acclaimed realist? When you look at the jar, is it half full or half empty?

*"There are only two kinds of people in this world—
the realists and the dreamers. The realists know where
they're going. The dreamers have already been there."*[2]

ROBERT ORBEN

One of the qualities I love most about Greg is his ability to see beyond the here-and-now. He's a risk-taker, a visionary. He welcomes change and isn't afraid of a challenge. He dreams big dreams and laughs heartily in the face of adversity.

Today, most of my friends would describe me similarly. But I doubt they would have when Greg and I first met. Fifteen years ago I prided myself on being a "realist," a word pessimists use to excuse their doubt.

"I decided to start a lead-generation business," Greg said, smiling.

"Oh, yeah?" My stomach immediately knotted inside me. I soon began firing off every thought in my mind. "Where are you going to put it? Who's going to manage it? How much will it cost?"

I'm not sure I even took a breath before I rattled on, "Where will you get your data? Where will you get the money? Will this conflict with your insurance company? Are you sure you really want to do this?"

Greg probably said to himself, *Well, I thought I was, but now I'm not so sure!*

In the early years of our marriage, I felt compelled to help Greg think through every detail surrounding his choices. I laid out every option before he could make any decision. Honestly, I'm not sure we would have ever arrived at a restaurant for dinner if it had been up to me; I may still be sitting in our car listing all the possible options.

For some reason, I felt it was my responsibility to strategically discover and point out any and every possibility for failure.

"Have you considered . . . How about . . . What if . . ." My concerns never stopped.

Thankfully, over the years, I've converted. I'm now an all-in kind of girl! Optimistic! Enthusiastic! Expectant! Honestly, I love the transformation of my thinking. I love believing for the best. I enjoy not living confined or limited to others' assertions of the impossible. I'm not sure exactly where the change began, but God radically changed my mindset from a scarcity to an abundance belief system. I wish I'd known this secret long ago: You get what you expect!

A Powerful Truth
Secret #10—You get what you expect.
So believe for the best!

On more than one occasion Greg's father said, "Son, you can have anything in this world you want. You just have to be willing to pay the price to get it."

What are you willing to give to stay in step with God's call?

God designed each one of us for a specific destiny. His Word says we were created on purpose for a purpose—one He decided long ago.[3]

Unfortunately, sometimes we sacrifice our destiny in exchange for immediate gratification. Early in the Bible we read, "Once when Jacob was cooking some stew, Esau came in from the open country, famished. He said to Jacob, 'Quick, let me have some of that red stew! I'm famished!' . . .

"Jacob replied, 'First sell me your birthright.'

"'Look, I am about to die,' Esau said. 'What good is the birthright to me?'

"But Jacob said, 'Swear to me first.' So he swore an oath to him, selling his birthright to Jacob.

"Then Jacob gave Esau some bread and some lentil stew. He ate and drank, and then got up and left.

"So Esau despised his birthright."[4]

When I first read this passage, I wondered: *How could someone be so shallow as to sell their birthright, their future blessing, their destiny, and the imminent favor of God for a bowl of soup? Seriously! A bowl of soup? Didn't Esau know he was destined for greatness? Didn't he understand the promise that awaited him? How could he possibly give up his blessing for such a simplistic thing?*

But as I contemplated Esau's actions, I realized various moments in my own life where I acted like Esau. I reflected on the times I gave up God's future blessing for my immediate relief, pleasure, or gratification.

Have you ever been lured from God's best in exchange for immediate money, love, or other self-indulgence? Have you ever caved in to the pressures of your circumstances and sought an easy-out? How about in marriage—have you ever discouraged your spouse from following God's call out of fear of the unknown?

Esau had an insatiable hunger for instant gratification. He wanted his immediate needs to be met, and in his impatience he sacrificed his future promise.

How about you? What presses in against you? What immediate gratifications cause you to want to give up God's future promise for immediate relief?

During the three-year stint of what I call Greg's and my dark season of the soul, God used our relationship to inspire one another to never quit. I remember one day when, tired and fatigued, I declared, "I can't do this anymore! I'm going to Fort Lauderdale tomorrow to interview for a pharmaceutical position."

"Oh, no, you are not!" Greg insisted. "We haven't endured all of this for you to give up now! If you get a job now, the last three years of our life will have been wasted."

One day I would talk Greg from jumping off the cliff; the next he would talk me off my window ledge. Back and forth, we reminded one another of God's call. Back and forth, we sought ways to inspire one another to dream. Back and forth, we dared to dream together.

Was it easy? Oh my goodness, no! Most days, it even felt impossible. But we pressed on, together. And that's the key—dare to dream, *together*!

I've watched too many friends begin well but not end well. As they've pursued their dreams, they've forgotten to pursue one another.

Sandy encouraged Ray to pursue his dream. She gladly delayed her degree so he could get his. Upon graduation, Ray got his long-awaited job, but it required him and Sandy to move five states from home. As the years went by, it always seemed like Ray faced just one more mountain to climb.

Over time, Ray became a little too important in his own mind. His ambition replaced his affection for Sandy. He failed to say thank you for her support. His appetite for success was never satisfied. Meanwhile, Sandy wondered, *Ray, do you even care for me? Have any of my sacrifices meant anything to you? What about my dreams?*

Twenty-seven years later, Sandy and Ray divorced. Ray's ambition still steals all of his energy, leaving him little time for anything but work. Sandy tries to fill her emptiness with more décor for her awarded two-story house. She wonders, *Where did it all go wrong?*

Emilie published book after book and won one award after another. Churches and businesses sought Emilie to speak for their conference events and business meetings. For a little while, she and her husband, Bryce, seemed like the ideal couple. Bryce was known for his magnetism and take-charge approach. Like Emilie, Bryce was widely in demand. Leaders from several nations sought his counsel, requiring him to travel frequently.

Eventually, Bryce's late-night business meetings turned into all-night parties. Warning signs popped up everywhere, but neither Emilie nor Bryce stopped pursuing their dreams. Both held fast to their individual ambitions, and so they compromised their relationship. Their dreams ran fast and furious but in separate directions that eventually pulled them apart.

As I've watched wonderful, dear friends and all-around really good people endure the pain of separation, I've become extremely conscientious to pray this prayer: "Lord, never give me more success than my character or family can sustain."

Lest I sound too saintly . . . let me say that I know my weaknesses. I know my longing for significance. I know my Type-A tendencies along with my insecurities. And so I pray, "Lord, save me from my own selfishness. May I never run ahead of You out of ambition, nor lag behind You out of fear. Instead, keep me by Your side, humbly following wherever You lead me."

I am so very grateful that Greg inspires me never to give up. He sacrifices his immediate gratification to encourage me to dream big. He offers me encouragement and communicates absolute belief in me, even when I doubt myself. He reminds me that God will fulfill all He has promised me. And I am committed to doing the same! That's why it works. God causes me to want to ensure that Greg's dreams happen, and He causes Greg to desire to see me embrace mine.

How about you? Do you dream with your spouse? Do you look for opportunities to encourage them to follow their God-given dreams?

Think back to when you first married. What dreams did you share? What did your future look like? Have you stopped dreaming together?

If so, realize that you can begin again. Invite your spouse to consider the following thoughts and to spend time answering the following questions.

Questions to Ask

1. In his book *Put Your Dreams to the Test,* Dr. John C. Maxwell stresses the importance of discovering if your dream is really *your* dream. He poses four questions to help readers discern if they are following their dream or someone else's: "What would I do if I had no limitations? What would I do if I had only five years to live? What would I do if I had unlimited resources? What would I do if I knew I couldn't fail?"[5]

2. Les Brown frequently says, "Shoot for the moon. Even if you miss, you'll land among the stars."[6] Do you encourage your spouse to shoot for the moon? Do you inspire their imagination? Ask them, "What do you think God wants for our lives? How can we move toward God's calling together? If given the opportunity what do you want to accomplish in life?"

3. Apple co-founder Steve Jobs once said, "Your time is limited, so don't waste it living someone else's life."[7] Have you given up dreaming because of the demands of life? How can you begin to responsibly, yet unmistakably and unreservedly, follow your God-given dreams? How can you encourage your spouse to do the same?

Verses to Consider

1. Proverbs 20:5 says, "The purposes of a man's heart are deep waters, but a man of understanding draws them out." Ask yourself: "What keeps me from daring to dream with my spouse? What actions can I take to demonstrate my belief in my spouse? How can I inspire them to pursue their God-given purpose?"

2. Second Corinthians 10:3-5 says, "For though we live in the world, we do not wage war as the world does. The weapons we fight with are not the weapons of the world. On the contrary, they have divine power to demolish strongholds. We demolish arguments and every pretension that sets itself up against the knowledge of God, and we take captive every thought to make it obedient to Christ." Scripture commands us to focus our minds on Christ. So ask yourself: "Do I demolish every pretension opposing God's truth? What attitudes do I communicate to my spouse? Am I influencing our relationship positively? How have my thoughts affected my spouse, our relationship, and our dreams?" *Trying — to encourage rather than discourage.*

3. Ecclesiastes 4:12 states, "Though one may be overpowered, two can defend themselves. A cord of three strands is not quickly broken." How have you severed or compromised the strength of your relationship with your spouse or with God? Have you committed and contributed to the strength of your marriage? Have you given your spouse the support they need, or taken time to dream with them about their dreams?

Greg's Turn

As a kid I dreamed of being a superhero. I tied a blanket around my neck and jumped off the footstool, pretending to save the day. "There's no need to fear; Underdog is here!" Sweet Polly Purebred and the rest of the world were safe so long as I was on the scene. If things got a little tough, I knew the simple fix: Just open the secret compartment of the Underdog ring and take a Super Underdog Energy Pill. Simon Bar Sinister, Rip Rap, and the gang were in a heap of trouble! Oh, how simple the world was back then.

Real life is different, isn't it? There are no magic pills to solve our problems when we're beat up. Encouragement often lingers far from us when we need it the most. To be our best, we need energy and encouragement from the people surrounding our lives.

As spouses, we possess the power to build or smash the dreams of our loved ones. Jim Rohn said, "We are the average of the five people we spend the most time with."[8]

In difficult seasons, it's easy to find naysayers. In fact, it's easy to be one and not even mean to. Some might say naysaying is part of our nature. Years ago researchers did a study with monkeys. Five monkeys were put in a room. No, they weren't jumping on a bed, but as the story goes, they may have bumped their heads! In the room was a banana tied to the ceiling. Underneath the banana was a ladder. The first monkey stepped up and eagerly climbed the ladder to get his prized banana. Just before reaching it, the researchers doused him with cold water. They also doused the monkeys who weren't climbing. One by one, each monkey attempted to climb to retrieve the banana. But over and over, every monkey was doused with cold water. It wasn't long until the monkeys pulled down any monkey attempting to climb the ladder and stopped them from even trying.

Okay—now here is where it gets interesting! The researchers replaced one of the monkeys with an inexperienced monkey. Sure enough, the newbie climbed the ladder, eyes fixed on the banana—but to no avail; the other monkeys attacked and pulled him down before he could reach it. This process continued until the researchers replaced every monkey in the group, so that there were no monkeys in the room who had been doused with water. Nevertheless, each time a new monkey joined the crowd, the mob would pull him down, ensuring there was no banana feast. Interestingly, none of the monkeys knew *why* they were pulling the others down. It was just what they had always done. It was what they were programmed to do by the other monkeys.

I'll leave it to you to make the application. But I will ask: Do you dream? Do you encourage your spouse to dream? Do you dream together?

One of the things I love most about Julie is how she supports and encourages me and my dreams. When I get weary and begin to doubt, Julie doesn't douse me with cold water. She is my biggest cheerleader. She chooses to believe the best in me. She is a safe place for me to share my aspirations. Truthfully, we are both a great support to one another. We love to laugh and share our dreams together.

You know by now that we have faced some hard times. Everyone does. Julie and I decided there are enough other monkeys in the world who are happy to pull us down; we've decided to encourage one another to dream big and go for it! Together we have resolved to be in a place where our dreams can be brought to life.

Why would any of us ever do anything to discourage one another from doing, having, or becoming what God desires for us? Shouldn't we learn what one another's dreams are and boost each other to reach even higher? Why would we spend any amount of energy convincing one another to be "realistic"? Will Smith said, "Being realistic is the most commonly traveled road to mediocrity."[9]

So here is your chance! You have an opportunity to be your spouse's superhero. When's the last time you encouraged them to dream? Are you finding ways to lift them up and help make their dreams come true? If not, ask God to help you. When you seek after Him, He will show you how to, once again, dare to dream together.

A Letter from the Father

Dear Child,

Know this: I am able to do immeasurably more than all you could ever ask, think, or imagine.[10] If you ask Me for anything in accordance with My will, I will hear you and give whatever you ask in My name.[11] Fix your thoughts on Me.[12]

Ambition ruins many people.[13] They run after things that will never satisfy.[14] Guard your heart.[15] Pursue me, and I will give you everything you need.[16] I will fulfill all I've promised you.[17] But I won't give it all at once, lest your promise overtake and overpower you.[18] Because you love Me, I will protect you.[19] I will not give you more than you can handle.[20]

Trust Me.[21] Relinquish your dreams to Me.[22] Rest in My power.[23] Drink in My goodness.[24] My plans are perfect.[25] Don't make plans in your own wisdom; instead listen intently for My instructions.[26] Don't weary yourself by trying to accomplish things in your own power; instead, follow closely and walk in steps of obedience.[27]

Who parted the Red Sea? Moses? No, but Moses witnessed My faithfulness and felt the limitlessness of My power when he obediently outstretched his hand toward it.[28] My purpose will be accomplished. My plans for your life will be fulfilled.[29] You only need to rest and watch My deliverance, being careful to do all I have called you to do.[30]

Don't worry.[31] Don't fear.[32] My plans for you are good, and My mercy endures forever.[33]

With all My love,
Your Heavenly Father

Closing Prayer

Father, I desire to be all You want me to be. I aspire to be a good spouse. Enable me to support my spouse's dreams. Teach me how to encourage their heart. Help me not to be detached; rather, empower me to inspire. Let the words of my mouth be ones of blessings, not curses.

_____ [Say your spouse's name] is a great person with incredible gifts. Grant me wisdom to promote Your perfect will and plan for them. Cause me to see their strengths and express verbal praise over their life. You called me to be _____'s spouse. Don't allow me to be cynical. Correct me quickly. I never want to be guilty of pessimism. May I never detract from Your call on _____'s life.

No matter how outlandish their dreams may seem, guard my mouth. May I never sneer or mock the desires of their heart. Keep us from making bad decisions; direct us in all of Your ways. Make our marriage thrive.

I pray in Jesus' name. Amen!

For Your Reflection

You get what you expect—so, believe for the best. But not just for *your* best; believe and dream for God's best *with* your spouse!

A Practical Application

I once read about a trainer who conditioned fleas to remain trapped inside an uncovered glass. Originally, the trainer trapped the flea by covering the glass jar with a lid. Each time the flea jumped, it met the resistance of the lid. Eventually the trainer removed the lid because he had effectively conditioned the flea to jump only so high. The flea remained confined to the glass because of its conditioning. Experience held the flea captive, though freedom was only a hop away.

Do past failures condition and limit you? Do you stay confined to a jar even though God has long removed the lid from it? Have you given up hope because of so many previous failed attempts?

How about for your marriage? Has society conditioned you to live with a shallow relationship?

Don't remain conditioned by past failures. You may discover, when you try again, that your glass has no lid. Foster a culture within your marriage whereby you share your dreams in a life-giving atmosphere:

1. Dare to laugh, love, and dream with the person God gave to you in marriage.
2. Season your words with life, such as: "I believe in you. With God's help, I know you can do it. You will succeed. God won't let you down. You can trust God. You are amazing. If anyone can do it, I know you can."
3. Find reasons to succeed instead of all the possibilities of failure. Instead of asking, "Will this work?" ask, "Why not? Let's do it!"
4. Provide solutions to assist in fulfilling one another's dreams, rather than pointing out all the obstacles.
5. Be genuine in your praise.

6. Ask God for wisdom to know how to better assist your spouse.
7. Write down your dreams individually and as a couple. Discuss what you can actively do to help one another's dreams come true.
8. Devise a plan together. Put timelines and deadlines to your dreams.
9. Revisit and talk about your hopes often. Chart your progress. Make any necessary changes. Always ask for God's wisdom.
10. Point to your spouse's successes. Remind them of their victories, and highlight their successful qualities.

Above all, remember this: *Transformation flourishes when we seek to promote another's happiness over our own.* Oswald Chambers wrote, "Never look for justice, but never cease to give it; and never allow anything you meet with to sour your relationship to men through Jesus Christ."[34]

As Christians, God requires us to love. Our love is a spiritual act of worship. True love expressed in marriage is mature, committed, and selfless. God charges both husband and wife to demonstrate their love for one another as He demonstrated His love. Do you want a thriving marriage? Every day, ask yourself, "How did Christ demonstrate His love for me? How can I demonstrate that kind of love to my spouse?"

Marriage offers us an amazing journey—one to be enjoyed and savored, not wasted. So join your hands with your spouse and dare to dream, believing for God's absolute best.

Appendix

10 Powerful Truths to Make Marriage Thrive

1. *Surrender to God, completely.*

2. *Forgive as God forgave you.*

3. *Don't shift the blame; take responsibility for your own actions.*

4. *Resist the devil's lies.*

5. *Understand the origin of one another's expectations and work to cultivate realistic expectations, together.*

6. *Control your tongue by allowing God to tame your heart.*

7. *Live intentionally to stay connected.*

8. *God wants you to say, "Yes!" to your spouse—to love them, body, mind and soul.*

9. *Fight for, not with, your spouse.*

10. *You get what you expect—so believe for the best.*

ADDITIONAL RESOURCES

Books

Allender, Dan. *The Wounded Heart.* Colorado Springs: NavPress, 1990.

Anderson, Neil T. *Victory over the Darkness.* Ventura, Calif.: Regal, 2000.

Arthur, Kay. *A Marriage Without Regrets.* Eugene, Ore.: Harvest House, 2000.

Arthur, Kay. *The Truth About Sex.* Colorado Springs: Waterbrook, 2005.

Brother Lawrence. *The Practice of the Presence of God.* New Kensington, Penn.: Whitaker, 1982.

Chambers, Oswald. *My Utmost for His Highest.* Westwood, N.J.: Barbour and Company, 1935.

Chapman, Gary. *The Five Love Languages.* Chicago: Northfield, 1995.

Downs, Tim and Joy. *The Seven Conflicts.* Chicago: Moody, 2003.

Dillow, Linda, and Pintus, Lorraine. *Intimate Issues.* Colorado Springs: Waterbrook, 1999.

Ethridge, Shannon. *Every Woman's Marriage.* Colorado Springs: Waterbrook, 2006.

Feldhahn, Shaunti. *For Women Only: What You Need to Know About the Inner Lives of Men.* Sisters, Ore.: Multnomah, 2004.

Gorman, Julie. *What I Wish My Mother Had Told Me About* Men. Franklin, Tenn.: Authentic, 2013.

Maltby, Tammy. *Lifegiving.* Chicago: Moody, 2002.

Maxwell, John C. *Becoming a Person of Influence.* Nashville: Thomas Nelson, 1997.

Maxwell, John C. *Put Your Dream to the Test.* Nashville: Thomas Nelson, 2009.

Morley, Patrick. *Devotions for Couples.* Grand Rapids, Mich.: Zondervan, 1994.

Murphey, Cecil. *Knowing God, Knowing Myself.* Ventura, Calif.: Regal, 2010.

Murray, Andrew. *Humility: the Journey Toward Holiness.* Minneapolis: Bethany, 2001.

Murray, Andrew. *Absolute Surrender.* Fort Washington, Pa.: Christian Literature Crusade, 1988.

Omartian, Stormie. *The Power of a Praying Wife.* Eugene, Ore.: Harvest House, 1997.

Parrott, Les and Leslie. *Relationships.* Grand Rapids, Mich.: Zondervan, 1998.

Rainey, Dennis and Barbara. *Moments with You.* Ventura, Calif.: Regal, 2007.

Rainey, Dennis and Barbara. *Rekindling the Romance: Loving the Love of Your Life.* Nashville: Thomas Nelson, 2004.

Swindoll, Charles R. *Hope Again.* Dallas: Word, 1996.

Warren, Rick. *The Purpose-Driven Life.* Grand Rapids, Mich.: Zondervan, 2002.

Organizations

FYI—For Your Inspiration. Learn more about FYI at: www.fyinspiration.org. Or, if you would like to schedule individual, group, or executive coaching with Greg and Julie Gorman, email FYI at: info@fyinspiration.org.

Focus on the Family: www.focusonthefamily.com.

Freedom in Christ Ministries, Dr. Neil T. Anderson: www.ficm.org.

New Life Ministries, Stephen Arterburn: www.newlife.com

Pure Life Ministries: www.purelifeministries.org

Wounded Heart Ministries, Dr. Dan Allender:
http://theallende rcenter.org.

ENDNOTES

A Note from the Authors
1. Matthew 12:20
2. Psalm 34:18

Chapter 1—Surrender, Completely
1. www.goodreads.com/quotes/tag/surrender
2. Daniel 3:16-18 emphasis added
3. Oswald Chambers, *My Utmost for His Highest* (Westwood, N. J.: Barbour, 1935), 31 May.
4. Rick Warren, *The Purpose Driven Life* (Grand Rapids, Mich.: Zondervan, 2002), 83.
5. www.goodreads.com/quotes/tag/surrender
6. Stephen R. Covey, *The 7 Habits of Highly Effective People.* (New York: Free Press, 2004), 43.
7. Charles R. Swindoll, *Hope Again* (Dallas: Word, 1996), 110.
8. Sandra Aldrich, *Men Read Newspapers, Not Minds* (Wheaton, Ill.: Tyndale, 1996), 83.
9. Andrew Murray, *Absolute Surrender* (Fort Washington, Penn.: Christian Literature Crusade, 1988), 37.
10. Dennis and Barbara Rainey, *Moments with You* (Ventura, Calif.: Regal, 2005), 17.
11. www.thefreedictionary.com/surrender
12. Oswald Chambers, *The Complete Works of Oswald Chambers* (Grand Rapids, Mich.: Discovery, 2000), 20-21.
13. Hebrews 4:13
14. Isaiah 41:10; 46:13
15. Hebrews 4:13; John 1:43-51
16. Hebrews 3:15
17. Matthew 11:28-30
18. Proverbs 3:5-6
19. Matthew 11:28-30
20. Isaiah 42:5

21. Psalm 136; Job 38
22. Daniel 6:22
23. Romans 8:28; 2 Peter 1:3
24. Mark 6:23; John 16:23
25. Psalm 100:5; 118:1; 136
26. Psalm 100:5; 118:1; 136
27. Matthew 7:9-11
28. Jeremiah 29:11-14

Chapter 2—Forgive, Completely
1. www.goodreads.com/quotes/tag/forgiveness
2. Matthew 6:15, Mark 11:26
3. Matthew 7:2, Luke 6:37
4. Shannon Ethridge, *Every Woman's Marriage* (Colorado Springs: Waterbrook, 2006), 38.
5. Neil T. Anderson, *The Bondage Breaker* (Eugene, Ore.: Harvest, 1990), 195.
6. Stormie Omartian, *The Power of a Praying Wife* (Eugene, Ore.: Harvest, 1997), 145.
7. Julie Gorman, *What I Wish My Mother Had Told Me About Men*, (Franklin, Tenn.: Authentic, 2013), 149.
8. Aldrich, *Men Read Newspapers, Not Minds*, 83.
9. Omartian, *The Power of a Praying Wife*, 144.
10. Les and Leslie Parrott, *Relationships* (Grand Rapids, Mich.: Zondervan, 1998), 20.
11. Luke 23:34
12. Chambers, *The Complete Works of Oswald Chambers*, 15.
13. Psalm 55:22; 1 Peter 5:7
14. Romans 8:15; Psalm 34:15; Hebrews 4:16
15. Ephesians 4:32; Colossians 3:13
16. Psalm 27:5; 31:20; 91:1
17. Isaiah 51:1
18. Romans 8:1; Isaiah 61:1-3

19. 1 Peter 5:10
20. 1 John 4:18
21. Romans 5:3-5
22. Genesis 50:20; Romans 8:28
23. Matthew 16:24
24. James 4:8
25. 2 Corinthians 5:17; Ephesians 2:1-10
26. Zechariah 4:6
27. 1 John 3: 5-6
28. 1 Peter 4:13; 2 Corinthians 1:5; Romans 8:17
29. Jeremiah 31:3

Chapter 3—Don't Shift the Blame
1. Tammy Maltby, *Lifegiving* (Chicago: Moody, 2004), 54.
2. John 10:10
3. www.goodreads.com/quotes/tag/blame
4. www.goodreads.com/work/quotes/2370171-how-to-win-friends-and-influence-people
5. www.goodreads.com/quotes/556851-direction-not-intention-determines-your-destination
6. Swindoll, *Hope Again,* 103.
7. Andrew Murray. *Humility: The Journey Toward Holiness* (Minneapolis: Bethany, 2001), 17.
8. www.proverbsway.com/2013/07/08/hands-down-the-top-15-quotes-by-oswald-chambers
9. Ephesians 5:25
10. Colossians 3:19
11. Matthew 5:44
12. Matthew 5:44
13. Luke 6:27-28
14. Colossians 3:13
15. John 13:34
16. Isaiah 53:6-12
17. Matthew 12:36; Romans 14:12; 2 Corinthians 5:10
18. James 4:10; 1 Peter 5:6
19. James 5:16; 1 John 1:9
20. John 13:35
21. Proverbs 15:1
22. Deuteronomy 31:6

23. Deuteronomy 31:6-8
24. Psalm 37:5-7
25. Exodus 14:14
26. Isaiah 49:23
27. Isaiah 66:2; Hebrews 4:16

Chapter 4—Resist the Devil's Lies
1. http://quotationsbook.com/quote/43070/
2. Ephesians 2:8-9
3. Psalm 103:12
4. Isaiah 49:16
5. http://christian-quotes.ochristian.com/christian-quotes_ochristian.cgi?query=lies&action=Search&x=0&y=0
6. John 10:10
7. Dennis and Barbara Rainey, *Rekindling the Romance: Loving the Love of Your Life* (Nashville: Thomas Nelson, 2004), 296
8. 1 Corinthians 13:5
9. http://johnmaxwellonleadership.com/2013/02/19/managing-the-disciplines-of-relationship-building/
10. Luke 23:34
11. Chambers, *The Complete Works of Oswald Chambers,* 31.
12. See Isaiah 43:7; Psalm 19
13. See Proverbs 5:15-19
14. See Matthew 5:28
15. See Philippians 2:3-4
16. See Matthew 19:6; Mark 10:9
17. Omartian, *The Power of a Praying Wife,* 18.
18. www.goodreads.com/work/quotes/2370171-how-to-win-\friends-and-influence-people
19. www.goodreads.com/author/quotes/1069006.C_S_Lewis
20. www.goodreads.com/work/quotes/2370171-how-to-win-
21. friends-and-influence-people
22. See 1 Peter 3:7
23. Ephesians 5:4
24. Matthew 5:28
25. Numbers 12:6; Proverbs 8:33
26. 1 Peter 5:8; James 1:14
27. 2 Corinthians 11:14; John 8:44

28. Proverbs 14:12; Proverbs 16:25
29. Psalm 37:5
30. Mark 9:7; Luke 9:35
31. Proverbs 8:17; Amos 5:4
32. Ezekiel 11:19; 36:26
33. Job 12:13; 28:20-23; 28:28; Psalm 111:10; Proverbs 2:6, 10
34. Psalm 37:4; 112:1
35. 1 Samuel 15:22; Psalm 149:4
36. Zephaniah 3:17
37. Jeremiah 29:11; John 7:38
38. John 16:33
39. Matthew 16:24-26; Psalm 149:4; 86:15; 1 Corinthians 10:13; Psalm 16:11

Chapter 5—Replace Unrealistic Expectations

1. Murray, *Humility: The Journey Toward Holiness*, 17.
2. Aldrich, *Men Read Newspapers, Not Minds*, 72.
3. Aldrich, *Men Read Newspapers, Not Minds*, 90.
4. Omartian, *The Power of a Praying Wife*, 40.
5. www.goodreads.com/quotes/tag/expectations?page=2
6. Tim and Joy Downs, *The Seven Conflicts* (Chicago: Moody, 2003), 40.
7. Acts 1:8
8. Jeremiah 29:13
9. James 4:6, 10
10. Ephesians 4:2
11. Ephesians 4:3
12. Psalm 16:11
13. 1 Peter 3:11-12
14. 2 Corinthians 10:5
15. Psalm 119:6
16. Psalm 1:1-3
17. John 13:14-17
18. 2 Timothy 3:1-5
19. Proverbs 14:12
20. John 6:63, 68; Isaiah 55:11
21. Luke 9:23-24

Chapter 6—Tame Your Tongue

1. Cited in Parrott, *Relationships*, 107.
2. Patrick Morley, *Devotions for Couples* (Grand Rapids, Mich.: Zondervan, 1994), 60.

3. Gary Chapman, *The Five Love Languages* (Chicago: Northfield, 1995), 45.
4. Patrick Morley, *Devotions for Couples*, 60.
5. Psalm 81:8
6. Psalm 46:10
7. James 4:8
8. Jeremiah 1:5-7; 2 Corinthians 5:17; Revelation 2:17
9. Isaiah 55:1-3
10. John 16:33
11. John 14:16, 26
12. Proverbs 19:11; Romans 15:7; Ephesians 4:2
13. Colossians 3:12
14. Luke 6:45; Proverbs 4:23; Matthew 12:34
15. Matthew 6:19-21; Psalm 19:9-10; Proverbs 16:16; 3:13-15
16. Matthew 11:29
17. 2 Corinthians 12:9-11; Zechariah 4:6
18. Romans 8:37;1 Corinthians 15:57; 2 Corinthians 2:14; Galatians 2:20
19. Jeremiah 33:6; Romans 8:5; Galatians 5:22
20. Psalm 65:3; Ephesians 4:32
21. Romans 12:9
22. Hosea 2:19-20
23. Jeremiah 3:14
24. Matthew 19:5-6; Mark 10:9
25. John 14:1, 27
26. Romans 9:33; 10:11; Isaiah 28:16; Jeremiah 17:7-8; John 7:38-39

Chapter 7—Be Intentional

1. Deborah Smith Pegues, *30 Days to Taming Your Fears: Practical Help for a More Peaceful and Productive Life* (Eugene, Ore.: Harvest, 2011), 89.
2. Cindi and Hugh McMenamin, *When Couples Walk Together: 31 Days to a Closer Connection* (Eugene, Ore.: Harvest, 2012), 11.
3. Dennis and Barbara Rainey, *Rekindling the Romance: Loving the Love of Your Life* (Nashville: Thomas Nelson, 2004), 35.
4. http://johnmaxwellonleadership.com/2009/08/21/todays-daily-reader-put-others-first/

5. *Vine's Expository Dictionary of Biblical Words* (Nashville: Thomas Nelson, 1985).
6. Shaunti Feldhahn, *For Women Only* (Sisters, Ore.: Multnomah, 2004), 27.
7. www.thefreedictionary.com/thoughtfulness
8. Isaiah 40:28-31; Hebrews 4:9-11; Matthew 11:28
9. Psalm 46:10
10. Proverbs 28:26; 26:11
11. James 4:13
12. John 15:16; Ephesians 2:10
13. 1 Thessalonians 5:9
14. Psalm 29:11; Isaiah 61:10; John 14:27
15. Luke 10:38-42
16. John 15:12; 13:34
17. Isaiah 66:2; Psalm 55:19; 1 Peter 5:5
18. Joshua 24:15
19. Psalm 32:8; Isaiah 58:11; Deuteronomy 31:8
20. Ezekiel 36:26
21. 2 Chronicles 16:9
22. Matthew 16:25; Luke 9:24; Matthew 10:39; Mark 8:35
23. Galatians 6:7

Chapter 8—Pursue Intimacy, Not Just Sex

1. Dagmar O'Connor, *How to Make Love to the Same Person for the Rest of Your Life.* (New York: Bantam, 1985), 293.
2. Patrick Morley, *Devotions for Couples,* 102.
3. Kay Arthur, *The Truth About Sex* (Colorado Springs, Waterbrook, 2005), 18.
4. Patrick Morley, *Devotions for Couples,* 118.
5. Shaunti Feldhahn, *For Women Only,* 93.
6. http://www.goodreads.com/work/quotes/14816053-the-four-loves
7. www.blazinggrace.org/porn-statistics
8. www.blazinggrace.org/porn-statistics
9. Cecil Murphey. *Knowing God, Knowing Myself* (Ventura, Calif.: Regal, 2010), 205.
10. Shaunti Feldhahn, *For Women Only,* 118.
11. Kay Arthur, *A Marriage Without Regrets* (Eugene, Ore.: Harvest, 2000), 161.

12. Napoleon Hill, *Think and Grow Rich: Your Key to Financial Wealth and Power.* (Success Co., 2009), 165.
13. Hill, *Think and Grow Rich: Your Key to Financial Wealth and Power,* 169.
14. Hill, *Think and Grow Rich: Your Key to Financial Wealth and Power,* 169.
15. Zephaniah 3:17
16. James 4:8
17. Psalm 50:15; Jeremiah 29:12; 33:3
18. Genesis 2:24-25
19. Proverbs 5:18
20. Song of Solomon 1:4
21. Ephesians 5:33
22. Matthew 19:6; Mark 10:9; Acts 10:15
23. Proverbs 5:17-18
24. Hebrews 13:4
25. Proverbs 5:18
26. Proverbs 5:19; Song of Solomon 7:10-12
27. 1 Corinthians 13:4-13; Colossians 3:14
28. Matthew 19:6; Mark 10:9
29. Ephesians 4:2
30. Proverbs 10:12; Ephesians 4:32; Colossians 3:13
31. Philippians 2:3-4
32. Song of Solomon 1:1-4; 1 Corinthians 7:3-5
33. Genesis 1:27-31

Chapter 9—Fight For, Not With, One Another

1. www.goodreads.com/quotes/495851-if-you-can-t-fly-run-if-you-can-t-run-walk
2. Murray, *Humility: The Journey Toward Holiness.* 17.
3. Downs, *The Seven Conflicts,* 62.
4. http://www.ask.com/question/who-many-light-bulbs-did-thomas-edison-do-before-finding-on-that-worked
5. Chambers, *The Complete Words of Oswald Chambers,* 51.
6. Isaiah 30:21
7. 1 Timothy 6:13
8. Isaiah 46:4
9. Isaiah 41:10
10. Nehemiah 9:6
11. Revelation 22:13

12. Genesis 26:24
13. Genesis 28:15
14. Isaiah 46:4
15. Isaiah 30:21
16. Haggai 1:13
17. Jeremiah 32:17; Luke 1:37
18. Hebrews 4:13
19. 1 Corinthians 2:9
20. 1 Corinthians 2:9
21. Exodus 33:14; Matthew 11:28
22. Psalm 37:23; Proverbs 3:5-6
23. Matthew 6:25-34
24. John 10:27-30
25. 2 Timothy 2:13
26. Acts 1:8
27. John 14:16-26;15:26; 16:7
28. Psalm 85:8; Isaiah 66:12
29. Deuteronomy 7:6-8; Isaiah 43:25; 63:9

Chapter 10—Dare to Dream, Together
1. www.en.wikipedia.org/wiki/
   Four-minute_mile
2. Dr. John C. Maxwell, *Put Your Dream to the Test* (Nashville: Thomas Nelson, 2009), xxii.
3. Ephesians 2:10
4. Genesis 25:29-34
5. Maxwell, *Put Your Dream to the Test,* 21.
6. www.goodreads.com/quotes/
   4324-shoot-for-the-moon-even-if-you-miss-you-ll-land
7. www.quotationspage.com/
   quote/38353.html
8. www.businessinsider.com/
   jim-rohn-youre-the-average-of-the-five-people-you-spend-the-most-time-with-2012-7

9. www.searchquotes.com/quotation/
   Being_realistic_is_the_most_commonly_traveled_road_to_mediocrity./
   323432/
10. Ephesians 3:20; Isaiah 58:11
11. 1 John 5:15
12. Hebrews 3:1
13. Luke 9:25; 1 John 2:16; 1 Timothy 6:9
14. Isaiah 55:1-3
15. Proverbs 4:23
16. Matthew 6:33
17. Genesis 28:15
18. Exodus 23:30; Deuteronomy 7:22
19. Psalm 91:14
20. 1 Corinthians 10:13
21. Psalm 37:5
22. James 4:13
23. 2 Corinthians 12:9
24. John 4:14
25. Romans 12:2
26. James 4:13; Proverbs 3:5-6;
    Romans 10:17; 8:28
27. Matthew 11:29; Isaiah 40:31;
    John 14:23-24
28. Exodus 14:21
29. Jeremiah 29:11; 1:5
30. Exodus 14:13-14; Joshua 1:7-9
31. Philippians 4:6-7; Matthew 6:25-34
32. Isaiah 41:10; Deuteronomy 31:6
33. Jeremiah 29:11; 1 Corinthians 2:9;
    Psalm 118; Psalm 136
34. Chambers, *The Complete Words of Oswald Chambers,* 16.